The GLORY OF ELECTRIC TRAMS

D.D. & J.M. Gladwin

THE OAKWOOD PRESS

© Oakwood Press 1993, D.D. Gladwin & J.M. Gladwin

ISBN 0 85361 453 9

Typeset by Gem Publishing Company, Brightwell, Wallingford, Oxfordshire.

Printed by Alpha Print (Oxon) Ltd, Witney, Oxfordshire.

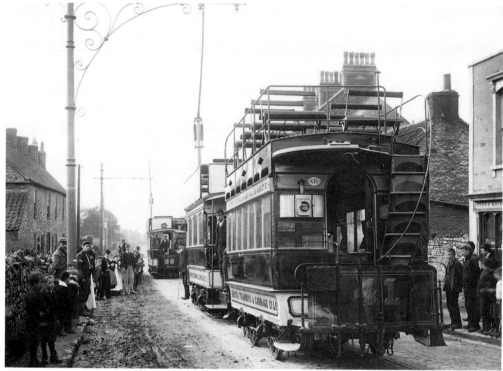

Probably the oldest photograph in the book, this is supposed to have been taken during October 1895 when the Bristol Tramways and Carriage Company opened their newly electrified line to Kingswood. Twenty-two power cars were purchased and many relatively new horse-tram cars were utilised as trailers. Oddly new horse-cars were being purchased as late as 1898. The three bay design and 30 hp of the electric tram was very up-to-date in 1895, but the use of a trailer meant that average speeds increased only to 8 mph (13 kph) from the 6 mph (10 kph) of horse drawn vehicles. No 'decency' boards are fitted to the upper deck of the trailer and as ladies (although not women) of the period rarely showed an ankle let alone their legs they would not have travelled on top. As the trailers could not legally be propelled difficulties with 'running round' at the termini led to their use being discontinued before the outbreak of war. The side mounted trolleys on these early electric cars had exposed springs which not only became very dirty but dripped molten grease on the passengers and indeed by the 1930s Bristol trams had become set in a time-warp with cars almost unchanged from 1910; German bombing finished the Kingswood route on the night of 11–12th April, 1941.

Authors' Collection

Published by
The OAKWOOD PRESS
P.O.Box 122, Headington, Oxford.

Contents

Authors' Note

During the nurturing of any book various problems inevitably arise, some of which can be clarified by a study of documents and books but inevitably there comes a time when we have to go cap in hand to ask colleagues (busy enough with their own activities) for help, both in answering queries and lending illustrations; and almost without exception they turn up trumps. Thanks therefore to:

G.E. Baddesley; R.J. Buckley; W.A. Camwell; D. Coates; J.C. Gillham; W.J. Haynes; R.W. Kidner; M. Knowles; K. Lane; R. Ludgate; J. Manners; N. Miller; A. Packer, H.B. Priestley; G. Shuttleworth; D.G. Voice; N. Williams; J-J. Wright; Birmingham, Huddersfield and Torquay Central Libraries' staffs; A. Depledge, Managing Director, Blackpool Transport Services; Mrs R. Thacker, Librarian, Tramway Museum Society, Crich and many members of the Fylde Tramway Society; LCC Tramways Trust; Light Rail Transit Association; Tramway Museum Society and the Tramway & Light Railway Society; and to others, no less helpful, who prefer to stay anonymous. Photographs are credited where we know, or can track down or guess, the source but any missing copyright acknowledgements that are notified will gladly be corrected in a later edition.

It is always inferred, if not exactly stated, by the media that to be interested in tramways one has to be incredibly old and doddery. It is not so, of course. As we were saying to this young relative just the other day, it seems only a few weeks ago that we rode with the nice Mr Train on his Birkenhead Street Railway. We can remember what the horse did quite clearly.

Introduction

Once upon a time every respectable town had its own tramway. Then along came the oil interests whose machinations killed off tramways. That is the hoary legend. The truth is that small tramways came, most made a little money and might have made more had not World War I destroyed all forward planning. But this war led to shortages of the most basic materials, and no amount of ingenuity in repairing and patching could hide the fact that, by 1928, most of the 'tiddlers' had run their course of life. They were still using the original tramcars, often with bodies not only un-modernised but with wooden longitudinal seating. The cars, running on broken rails and over dropped joints, were regularly derailed when the cobbles higher than the track would lift and deflect the motor's casing. Each jolt aged worn bodywork and each jar increased the wear on motors, gears and tracks alike. Once these cars had been new and a matter for civic pride, now, worn, with faded paintwork and emitting a cacophony of sound, they were too slow and too uncomfortable to cope with the motor bus competition.

Another difficulty, not easily overcome, was that virtually all tramways were built on the back of borrowed money and while they were in profit the private companies collected their dividends as avidly as the Corporations (for various sociological and political reasons) used their profits to reduce fares. Little or no attempt was, or had been made, to establish a 'Sinking Fund' or piggy-bank to cover any bad times that might follow. Which towns were these? Sheerness, Neath, Taunton, Morecambe, Keighley, Kilmarnock, Wantage, Ipswich, the Hartlepools, Wrexham and Camborne, Glossop and Worcester and Matlock all, and many others, had lost their trams by 1928. And the slaughter continued, with the track of 36 companies and Corporations being lifted between 1928 and 1930 alone. Some of these maintained the electrical connection by substituting trolleybuses, especially where the distribution cables and, indeed, the generating station, were owned by the local councils. Darlington, Ipswich, the Hartlepools, Chesterfield and Wolverhampton, all followed this course – but Ramsbottom, rather oddly, had tried trolleys and abandoned them by 1931.

Gradually though, the emphasis did change, as once these worn-out anachronisms were eliminated, the bulk of the remaining tramways were efficient, well-maintained and provided an essential service. Probably they were uneconomic in today's terms inasmuch as they did not make a direct profit. But what the Birmingham, Sheffield, Leeds and Liverpool trams did was to allow the townsfolk who worked at the great factories, mills, docks, steelworks and mines to live away from their places of employment. The massive council estates of the 1930s were generally served by extensions of tramway routes or followed routes that had once been built as speculative ventures to quiet villages. Council rents helped the Corporation books to balance, industries rates and taxes brought in a vast income against which tramway losses were piffling.

But there was also an obverse to this coin: Birmingham, whose trams were not finally eliminated until 1953, bought no new cars (bar a couple of 'experimentals') from 1929; London (removed 1952) from 1933 when out of 2,560 cars only 20 per cent could be said to be modern. Leeds closed 1959, purchased its last new vehicles in penny packets and by 1945 their 400 cars had an average age of 20 years, although in fairness they did have a scheme to introduce Euro-type vehicles, experiments with single-deckers coming to fruition in 1953, but it is said they were unable to have them manufactured at an economic price.

A surprising number of Corporations made an attempt to introduce new-pattern vehicles, but only in relatively miniscule numbers. Belfast, whose magnificent system closed as late as February 1954 had superb McCreary streamline cars in service in 1935. But these only totalled 50 vehicles out of nearly 400 in service, and trams, like trains, can only go as fast as the slowest one on the line. Liverpool kept going until 1957 with many attractive 'modern' cars albeit most were built prior to the war and had stood up to the rigours of bombing, blast damage and even daylight machine-gunning. Darwen, closed 1946, had just two streamliners, while Manchester, incredibly advanced with their buses, had only 38 so-called 'Pilcher' 4-wheel cars of 1930 to represent modernity out of 952 cars. Even as late as 1937 when 735 cars remained, only 511 were regarded as being even remotely suitable for modernisation. The tramways of Manchester, like those of Bury, Blackburn and Rotherham, closed in 1949.

Whether or not the oil companies consciously influenced Town Hall decisions we shall probably never know, certainly there was anti-tram propaganda, but there was an equal belief that tower blocks represented the way forward for state-owned housing and that underpasses would resolve the dilemma of what to do with the pedestrian in the age of the motor car. You could not have trams and tower blocks and underpasses; they were simply incompatible and with their apparent lack of flexibility the rail-bound tram was seen as holding up progress. The same argument was also advanced against 'heavy' railways with the result that many lines and stations were eliminated. Thirty years later we are wiser and, to cite just one example, Birmingham, Snow Hill closed in 1968 has been re-opened and work is progressing to reinstate the link to the Kidderminster line. There are also plans to introduce three new Birmingham tramways, albeit based on Continental practice.

Having eliminated tramways, or so the theory went, cities could look forward to a great new future. Did something go wrong? As a tramwayman I saw Sheffield bustling with industry as we carried thousands of people to their places of employment. By any standards for those who could and would work there was prosperity based on honest industry. As a tramwayman I also saw Liverpool as a busy vigorous port with the tramcars hard pressed to move the numbers waiting to pay their coppers to our conductors, and I saw Glasgow, wet, grey and often bleak but fired with a sense of urgency that reflected the spirit of the town. Too young to work on London trams I remember the cheerfulness of their crews as the overloaded, creaking cars carried their passengers from suburbs to city in the dawn and back again in the evening.

When the trams went from the big cities, something died. And I'm told it was the same when the last antideluvian cars, still with the driver exposed to the elements and with no top covers, left Bristol. My wife has told me how Weston-super-Mare was suddenly a bewildering place to visitors, long accustomed to board the town's solid, respectable, trams to the sanatorium or beach or wherever they were pleased to go. Can one imagine Blackpool without its trams today? The truth is that the remaining line was very nearly closed in 1967 and there is still a strong caucus in the town who would consider it good if the streets were rid of the steel rails. Princes Street, Edinburgh, seemed wrong to me when I went back a few years ago – I still subconsciously hoped that maybe one of their, so beautiful, madder red cars would swish up and take me away to Annie's Cafe.

Once between Llandudno and Colwyn Bay neat single deck and well-maintained double deck cars carried holidaymakers and local alike to that charming line. It was closed following a relatively small financial loss, and the Council happily substituted buses. They were a disaster and eventually from something to be proud of, a tramway, the Council had only Crosville's buses. Portsmouth had a tramway, and so did Dover, Chatham, Grimsby, Immingham, Cardiff, Hull. Merchant and Royal Navies were well served in the days when British seamen served on British shipping. By contrast, customers of the Cruden Bay Hotel in Scotland were equally well served with their own tramway. Cork and York, Accrington and Rawtenstall, Gloucester and Great Yarmouth had one thing in common – trams. These carried the religiously inclined to their services and 'Instructions to Motormen' told the drivers not to ring their bells or make other excessive noise when the Divine Services were being held . . .!

In this book I have followed only one precept and that is of variety. Here are the latest streamliners, and the oldest open-toppers. Once in Aberdeen I saw the one behind the other and very odd it looked to. Here are single deck cars that were enormously long, and stubby little double-deckers. There are tramcars dressed in all their youthful finery, and sad tired tramcars defeated by too many years of service. There are cars on the day services began and, gloomily, a couple on their last days. There are bits of tramcars and a few of their crews – with ladies among them to grace the pages.

If a little of my enthusiasm shows through and influences you to take a trip to Blackpool and to ride on the trams there then that's a good act well done! For there you will find some trams of the 1930s that represented the most up-to-date styling of the time, you may see cars of the 1950s and certainly the boxy cars of the 1980s, attractive enough with a clean modern image. From time to time Blackpool entertains visiting trams loaned from Museums and marvellous they look earning their board and lodging. If you seek pure nostalgia then the Manx Electric Railway is there to be visited, including gorgeous single deck cars that hopefully will soon receive a birthday telegram from Her Majesty the Queen. For now read on, and join me in memories and dreams.

D.D. & J.H. Gladwin

Plate 1: In some respects it may seem a little odd to commence an overview of traditional tramways with a photograph of a modern Blackpool tram, and a single decker at that, but, in reality, No. 646 represents one step in a British evolutionary train whereas the new 'Metro' vehicles are a quite distinctive type of machine, betraying continental influence and manufacture.

The chassis and bogies of No. 646 were manufactured by the Primrose Three Axle Company of Blackburn; the motors are English Electric-built; the bogie frames come from Stress Free Plastics of Cleveleys and the bodywork is by East Lancashire (Coachbuilders) Ltd of Blackburn. These Centenary class cars, eight in all, have not been entirely successful but then it is almost impossible to find cars that did not undergo some modifications at some time. No. 646 entered service in 1988 and is a 53-seater, designed for economic one-person operation, particularly in winter. *Authors' Collection*

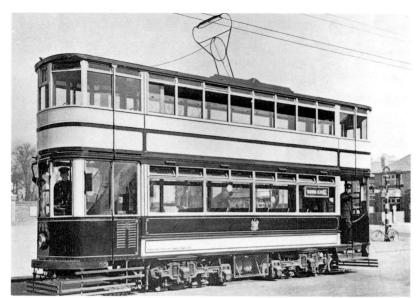

Plate 2: Birmingham Corporation Tramways would never have been called an adventurous concern, preferring instead to build on their achievements. They introduced bow collectors when it became apparent that they had – in a developed form and in certain locations – considerable advantages over the trolley pole; air brakes were gladly used when they became reliable and bogie improvements were continually being made. Car No. 792, seen here in May 1928 while still new, was one of a series of 50 cars and the Brush bodywork was chosen because their product was tried and tested. English Electric provided the electrical equipment and brakes came from the EMB Company as 'they had [previously] given every satisfaction'. Sixty-two seats in a narrow gauge tramcar was excellent, and in their artificially truncated 24 year life each car ran over 650,000 miles. Both driver and conductor look smart, reflecting the quiet pride of a Corporation employee. *Authors' Collection*

Plate 3: In the 1940s there were, thankfully, a number of enthusiasts who were dedicated enough to plod around, often with bulky all-manual cameras, on their one-day-a-week off and take photographs of the dying, disliked and despised means of transport – the tram. At Prescot, terminus of Liverpool's route 10, stands Liner (Green Goddess) No. 174, on 20th June, 1948. She is battered, grubby and drooping around the platforms but still gives a hint of how she looked when built in 1936, by the Corporation Tramways Department at Edge Lane Works. Containing 78 leather seats in a 36ft 9in. body and boasting 160 hp, they were real trams. No. 174 was burnt out on 27th April, 1954, having outlasted route 10 Prescot South Castle Street which closed on 26th June, 1949. *George Shuttleworth*

Plate 4: Doncaster's first tramway line was opened on 2nd June, 1902 and the last closed on 8th June, 1935, being replaced by trolleybus services. Trackwork was quite unusual insofar as centre-grooved rail was utilised, so that instead of the wheel-flange being on the inside of the wheel it was in the middle and the rails slotted accordingly. It was said that with two bearing surfaces rather than one, running was much smoother, although as only Hull used the same form of rail, they cost far more. This tramcar was built as an open-topper in 1903, and gained a prefabricated lid a few years later; it is seen on the Brodsworth route shortly after its opening on 21st February, 1916. The girls are war-time employees taken on to replace men serving in the trenches; as both conductors are fully kitted out we may assume another car was lurking behind the photographer; although not visible the headlight would be masked against Zeppelin attacks.
R.J. Buckley

Plate 5: How trams are remembered best by older folk really depends on where childhood memories were formed. Anyone less than 50 or so is unlikely to remember the long country routes, although even a mere stripling could reflect upon the reserved track sections of Liverpool, Sunderland and Birmingham. To a city dweller the memory is of tram-jams; like the common belief today that all BR trains are late so motorists believed that trams were stationary all the time.

The picture shows Leeds Corn Exchange in July 1932 and car No. 346 and her sisters awaiting departure. A few years later she was to have the upper deck enclosed but was soon relegated to peak hour and football services only.

Authors' Collection

Plate 6: Photographed from the balcony of the Paramount cinema in Newcastle (now the Odeon) in 1938, three cars from the tram fleet work down Northumberland Street *en route* to Heworth. Visible, too, are at least three of Newcastle's yellow trolleybuses and an amazing selection of other vehicles. Car No. 195 was one of class 'E', built between 1912 and 1914, and lasted almost unchanged until 1949.

Newcastle Chronicle & Journal

Plate 7: Photographed around 75 years ago, a traditional car, built in 1907, hisses along Bonhill Road, Dumbarton, *en route* to Dumbuck terminus. The silence of a tramcar in these snowy and windswept conditions could be quite unnerving to a passer-by, but their solid reliability regardless of almost any weather was one of their greatest assets. This photograph is quite evocative of the short period that Dumbarton's Tramways existed; cars Nos. 1–6 were delivered late, ran unchanged and, open vestibuled though they were, remained in service tatty and battered 'during the inclement season' until the cessation of services in March 1928. Their enclosed top decks made them at least endurable for passengers but drivers in their open cabs were not even issued with uniforms during the last year or two of services, many layers of newspapers and 'British Warm' soldiers' overcoats protecting them from the bitter wind.   *Authors' Collection*

Plate 8: The opening of a tramway, or a new line of tramway was an excuse both for the cars to be decorated and for the dignitaries to have free buns and biscuits, if not something more substantial.

On 31st October, 1905, opening day, car No. 1 is photographed at Perth depot waiting to enter service, with the Corporation Band meanwhile giving a 'selection of popular numbers'. Years later, the same car was to act as the vehicle of the war recruiting drive and was finally again illuminated to celebrate the end of the war.

At 2 pm precisely the Town Council and their guests left for the power station, then boarded two cars (including No. 1) in the High Street and were taken to be shown the latest 'civic adornment', the Depot at Scone. Patriotically, Perth ordered their 12 cars from Hurst Nelson of Motherwell and although tentative proposals were put forward to renew or refurbish these trams, they were scrapped more or less in the condition they had begun in; it is said three or four were never even repainted and by the end, 19th January, 1929, the bodies were rickety, noisy and 'noisome'. *Authors' Collection*

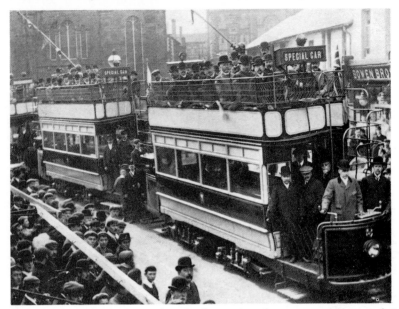

Plate 9: The intention in this book is to show the sheer variety of tramways and their cars that at one time operated in Great Britain with a glance, too, at foreign parts for their contrast. Here is shown the opening of Pontypridd's electric tram service at 11 am on 5th March, 1905. Not really much of a show and the numbers of bystanders were augmented by giving local schoolchildren a half-day holiday. Three cars were used to carry the dignitaries who, duty done, had a celebratory lunch and went home, public services commencing at 2 pm. *Authors' Collection*

Plate 10: Despite bitterly cold weather, the bowler hats are present for the great day, the opening of the City of Lincoln Tramways on 23rd November, 1905. So, too, are the local youth looking suspiciously clean. It is interesting to see how the constables appear to tower above the ordinary folk. This tramway system had two unusual attributes. The tramcars were painted a pale green and operated, not through orthodox overhead wires, but through a series of studs laid in the roadway. This, the Griffiths-Bedell surface contact system, was so designed that the studs were 'dead' until energised by a powerful magnet carried under each car. Night-time travel was, apparently, interesting, because although the usual dead spots between overhead feeds were eliminated, studs that did not work could plunge the car into darkness or, worse, if two of three 'died', could bring the tram to a fairly abrupt halt. In 1919, mainly due to a lack of spares for the stud system, orthodox overhead was installed and three new trams purchased; however the tramway closed in March 1929. *Authors' Collection*

Plate 11: The 3.78 miles of Ilkeston Corporation Tramways were not, by any standard, a successful investment. With hindsight one can look back and wonder why some of these town concerns were built; but small-town pride was great and, prior to World War I, even in these localities, home-longing was the paramount emotion. Services commenced on 16th May, 1903; the network was operated by the Nottinghamshire & Derbyshire Tramways Company from 1916, purchased by them in 1922 and finally expired in the dark days of winter on 7th February, 1931. Technically this is a poor photograph but has the great merit of being 'alive' with all the charm of a snapshot. It is salutory to reflect on the difficulties facing a cameraman 90 years ago, with a heavy mahogany box to be carried, and here lifted to head height, the glass slide requiring at least a two second time exposure.   *Authors' Collection*

Plate 12: Yorkshire (Woollen District) Electric Tramways commenced operating trams in 1903, the last car running in October 1934. Within the 'Heavy Woollen' manufacturing area of Yorkshire each council was once marked for its fierce parochialism. In many ways this was (and is) excellent but when this micro-patriotism spilled over into tramways life became complicated.

To give an example. This company ran trams from, in effect, Birkenshaw to Thornhill via Dewsbury, albeit, incredibly, in two parts. At Dewsbury the width of the market place kept away the cars of the Dewsbury, Ossett and Scothill Nether Company, who made an end-on non-physical connection with Wakefield & District trams at Ossett. These were all standard gauge (4 ft 8½ in.) tracks. At Birkenshaw the Woollen District company met the tracks of Bradford Corporation – but they were of 4 ft 0 in. gauge. In the midst of this, squarely in the middle of the Woollen District's 17 miles of track, Batley Corporation defiantly owned their own bit of trackwork and their own cars, painted green and white rather than the Company maroon and white. Buses recognise no boundaries and were to use this inherited weakness of tramways to eliminate them.

Here the first tram arrives at Comersal on 2nd October, 1903; holidays from school again, patriotism and some degree of enthusiasm are evident. The road surface shows just why tramways were so popular in early years.   *A.D. Packer Collection*

Plate 13: This illustration is the only one in this book of electric tramways to feature a horse. R.W. Kidner, doyen of tramway historians, describes the scene thus: 'I think this photo can only be the formal change of the former South East Metropolitan horse-bus route from Greenwich to Rushey Green, Catford, to electric trams on 10th June, 1906. The electric car could be a class 'B' or 'C'; 'B's got open-ended top covers in 1906 and 'C's in 1904; from 1907 they began to change to all-enclosed, so there is quite a narrow margin of dating. It is a very evocative photo'. We do not know who took their camera and recorded the scene, but this moment represented a whole change of life for this part of London. *Authors' Collection*

Plate 14: White-painted car No. 1931 of class 'E/3' was chosen for the opening ceremony (14th January, 1931) of the rebuilt Kingsway Tunnel which allowed for a direct cross-London tramway connection for the first time. The section of such a tunnel may not now seem at all large in comparison with recent developments, but car No. 1931 measured 15 ft 7½ in. from the railheads to the trolley plank, and to obtain clearance for both tram and the overhead through a London soil perforated by sewers, water and gas pipes plus electric cables, all of which required diversion, was really quite remarkable over 60 years ago. *Authors' Collection*

Plate 15: As built car No. 914 was one of 470 identical cars built during 1898–1901 for the electrification of Glasgow's tramways. Had the Corporation never added any further trams they would have been one of the largest operators, but as it was by the end of 1902 they had 681 (of various designs) in service, eventually rising to 1,208 in 1948.

As built No. 914 was open-topped, seating a nominal 25 on longitudinal wooden benches on the lower deck and 30 'outside' on transverse reversible wooden seats. By the beginning of World War I another 312 virtually identical 'standards' had been built, all by now with covered tops.

When women drivers were first employed they were provided with very fetching uniforms in 'Black Watch' pattern; but eventually this was superseded by the smart design shown here. Her police whistle was to warn horse-lorry drivers to vacate the tramlines which they preferred to use rather than the cobbles. Glasgow like many cities gladly employed the widows of any of its employees lost or seriously injured in the war; I was told that such a widow kept her husband's seniority.

The paintwork of the car is excellent (as most were even in their last days), and the construction details interesting. *D.H. Johnson*

Plate 16: No. 1293, the first of what should have been thousands, but instead only one of 100. Built at Coplawhill Works of Glasgow Corporation Tramways in 1948 (the last, No. 1392, left in 1952) and known as Coronation Mk.II; her alternative nickname of *Cunarder* seemed more appropriate for, at speed with the wind on their bows, her 144 hp caused a graceful shouldering movement for all the world like the *Queen Elizabeth* creaming her way across the North Atlantic. Dimensions were slightly different at 34 ft 6 in. long and 7 ft 3½ in. wide, seating 66 passengers in luxury, with moquette covered seats downstairs and leather upstairs. Running on a slightly unorthodox gauge of 4 ft 7¾ in., so designed that 'main line' railway stock could, and did, run along the tramway tracks, the electric tram commenced commercial service in Glasgow on 13th October, 1898 and finished long before it was desirable or even sensible, on 4th September, 1962. The photograph was taken at Rouken Glen on 11th August, 1953. The names of the driver and conductress are not known, the ticket machine is an 'Ultimate' and a very useful defensive weapon. *D.H. Johnson*

Plates 17 to 21: By the 1930s Manchester and Salford tended to have outwardly similar fleets of tramcars, much as the local councils around London used to follow the LCC pattern. In horse tram days one concern, the Manchester Carriage & Tramways Company, served both boroughs and, even after electrification, Manchester and Salford Corporation Tramways were physically connected in six places. Salford Tramways' first electric service commenced on 4th October, 1901, and the last traditional tram ran back to the depot on 31st March, 1947, while Manchester's equivalent dates were 3rd June, 1903 and 13th February, 1948. But these figures do not tell the whole story as both tramways had a pounding during the war and on both only minimal maintenance was carried out thereafter until closure; although one must add that had it not been for the war the end would have come sooner. The external and internal shabbiness of the cars at the end was in distinct contrast with those of Liverpool, Leeds or Sheffield which still looked capable of continuing forever.

Plate 17: Manchester's open balcony 4-wheeler No. 726 still retains some of the fancy paintwork Manchester Corporation Tramways Depot were famous for in the good days. Built in 1912 in the Tramways Workshops, and seen at Piccadilly 20 years later, she was the embodiment of a solid workmanlike tramcar.

In its heyday, Manchester had the third largest tram system in Great Britain, having 952 cars in service at one time and 123 miles of route. If we consider Salford to be a part of Manchester, then the combined tramway networks were second only to London. The crews are well dressed (sadly, towards the end, all too often they were not) and the guard is wearing his summer cap cover.

Authors' Collection

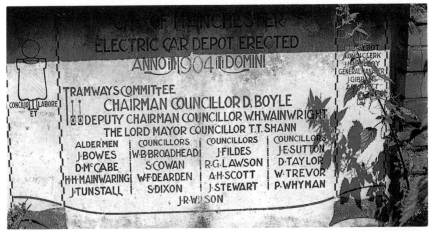

Plate 18: Nowadays, the chairpeople of transport corporations appear with a very few exceptions to be quite forgettable. Their names may appear on a plaque one day but this stone was ready and waiting when the new depot was opened. The General Manager's name appears in small print as he was merely an employee and in those robust days of civic pride there was no doubt over the gender of the members of the tramway committee.

Hyde Works officially opened in 1904 but was partially functional before this; it built its first tramcar bodies in 1907 and thereafter more or less continually until completion of the 'Pilcher' series of 1932.   *Authors Collection*

Plate 19: Bogie car No. 934 was built by English Electric, albeit to the Manchester Corporation Tramways Department's design; the affinity with, and progression from No. 726 is obvious. Of particular interest, and clearly visible in the photograph, are the bogies. Built by EMB specifically for Manchester Corporation Tramways, they were of the maximum traction type, said to give even distribution of the load onto the rails without loss of grip in poor conditions. Based on a very early Brill (American) pattern they were modified with an extra top bar and superior springing. Two 50 hp motors made this class of tram, seating 80, very fast where trackwork permitted. The scene is Parker Street, Piccadilly, in the late 1930s, the buildings on the right are in Portland Street and the spire behind the bus an 'architectural gem' above the Law Court. The bus with its rather fancy 'streamline' appearance is on route 50. Route 33A, a so-called 'short' working, ran between Reddish and Belle Vue.   *W.J. Haynes*

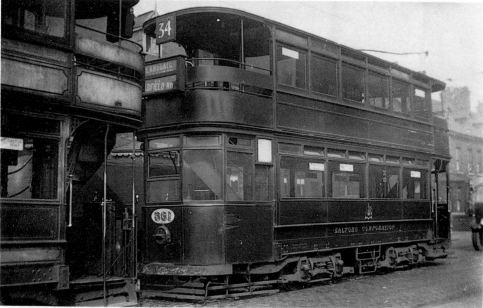

Plate 20 (opposite): Salford's No. 217, built in 1915, was photographed outside Weaste Depot on 31st March, 1947, having taken over from a failed No. 221 (hot axle box) in the final hours of tramway service; Weaste Depot had already officially closed on 3rd March. No. 217 drooped at one end, leaked, jangled and all the glass rattled as she went over each rail joint. Her neglected state was in marked contrast to the flashy replacement buses. *G. Shuttleworth*

Plate 21 (opposite): Salford's No. 361 was, by any standards, an old tramcar by 1946, having first been assembled as No. 124 in 1903. The top cover was added and some strengthening undertaken in 1924 and later she was renumbered. Psychologically, like changing the registration letter on a car, it helped to hide her true age! She is seen in wartime livery which she retained to the end. No. 223 in front, is in pre-war colours, combined with post-war decrepitude. The last Salford car in public service, No. 350, ran back to the depot on 31st March, 1947. *Authors' Collection*

Plate 22 (above): All the tramways around Manchester had one thing in common towards the end. They were pretty awful, and it is memories of rackety trackwork, bedraggled, weary cars and general neglect and grime that still stick in the minds of many people when they hear the word 'tram'.

Oldham Corporation's car No. 128, built as recently as 1926, looks worn and down-at-heel in this just post-war view. She was to be reprieved from the scrapyard being sold with another handful of Oldham cars to Gateshead, there receiving the number 70 in their fleet, and giving five years' further service. She is seen on route 20, Manchester–Waterhead, which was interworked with cars from Manchester Corporation Tramways. Oldham abandoned their remaining routes on 3rd August, 1946, when this through service was replaced by new Crossley motorbuses on service 98.

Authors' Collection

Plates 23 to 27: It is impossible to tell the story of Leeds tram services and their tramcars in a few lines, as in many ways their cars were advanced and yet they were bedevilled by one mistake; a mistake which the patrons were never to forget and which cost the tramway department money better spent elsewhere.

Socially Leeds was an advanced city building massive housing estates which, whatever their faults then and now, were far better than the slums they replaced. Moving people to the outskirts of the city created a demand for transport, which the tramways were flexible enough to undertake. New lines, often in reservations, were built, although as a trade-off 30 miles of lightly used line were closed between 1933 and 1938. Their mistake, made in all good faith, was to order 200 sets of the new EMB 'pivotal' truck for use with new tramcars. The objective was to have a high capacity, two motor car which would be able to utilise a long wheelbase truck – some 10 ft compared with the 5 ft 6 in. norm. The ride would be steady and the load spread more evenly so that the body would be less liable to racking, drooping and leaks. The idea was that each pair of wheels would be free to take the curve individually – in effect two single axle bogies. The problem put very simply was that as the wheel flanges wore or if the track was a little wide to gauge the wheels stuck at an angle and continued to try to go round a curve long after they should have been straight.

The racket was apparently appalling and, worse still, both the flanges and the rails wore out faster and so the wheels got even more confused until they took to the cobbles or broke. These cars, the 'Pivotals' cost, in round figures, £2,000 each, financed by a 20 year loan. As they were delivered from 1926 onward they had to be made to run without excessive extra cost at least until 1946.

Leeds City Tramways
and
Transport Department.

PARCELS SERVICE

BETWEEN

Leeds	Wakefield	Horbury	Ossett
Castleford	Knottingley	Normanton	
Pontefract	Hemsworth	Barnsley	

etc.

June 14/26.

Commencing on **Monday, November 2nd, 1925,** Parcels will be accepted by The Leeds City Tramways at any of their Depots for the above Districts, and others, enumerated on the handbills.

The undermentioned rates include delivery in Wakefield ~~only~~ *area*. Parcels intended for all ~~other~~ districts will be conveyed to the advertised Depots, ~~to be called for~~.

	On Tramcars. (Non Delivery).	Up Omnibuses.	Leeds and Wakefield. (Delivery included).
Parcels up to 7 lbs.	4d.	4d.	6d.
Exceeding 7 lbs. and not exceeding 14 lbs.	6d.	6d.	9d. *8*
„ 14 lbs. „ „ „ 28 lbs.	8d.	8d.	10d.
„ 28 lbs. „ „ „ 42 lbs.			1/-
„ 28 lbs. „ „ „ 56 lbs.	10d.	10d.	1/2
„ 56 lbs. „ „ „ 84 lbs.	Not carried	1/-	1/5 *1/6*
„ 84 lbs. „ „ „ 112 lbs.	„	1/6	1/8 *1/10*

2d. every additional 14 lbs.

(Trams only).

(On Buses and Trams).		
Small Hand Sewing Machines, 1/- each	Perambulators and Cabinet Sewing Machines	2/6 each.
	Stand Sewing Machines	3/- each.
	Bicycles	1/6 each.

ALL PARCELS MUST BE PREPAID, FULLY ADDRESSED AND WELL PACKED.

Parcels over 112 lbs. please divide.

Packages containing Furniture, Glass, China, Light Hardware or Fragile Goods are carried only at Owner's Risk, unless sufficiently packed and an extra 50 per cent. over ordinary rates paid.

A declaration is necessary at the time of despatch.

Live Stock, Explosives, Matches, Tins with " Let in Lids " (not soldered or otherwise securely fastened) and parcels of an objectionable nature or likely to damage others, not accepted.

Bulky parcels are subject to a slight extra charge.

List of Districts and Agents and all particulars can be had from The Parcels Office, King's Mills, Swinegate.

Contracts arranged.
Delivery within ½ a mile of Agent's premises.

W. CHAMBERLAIN,
General Manager.

Tel. No. 21601.

[P.T.O.

Jowett & Sowry Ltd., Leeds.

Plate 25: Towards the end of the 1940s Leeds Tramways faced a dilemma, one choice led to tram subways operated by single deck cars and the other was the road to oblivion. No. 600 was 'home grown', albeit based on Sunderland car No. 85. It was mounted on ex-Liverpool heavyweight EMB trucks, one of the sweetest runners ever, and entered service in August 1954, as a possible prototype or at least guinea pig for a future class of 'super trams' but three years later she was laid to one side.

Authors' Collection

Plate 26: As a tramway operator Leeds had a penchant for buying other companies' redundant vehicles and, indeed, by outlasting many of their contemporaries they were able to pick up some rare bargains. Pre-war they bought three London 'HR/2' class cars with more to follow although the war prevented further movement, then cars followed from Hull, Southampton, Manchester and, again during 1950, London in the form of 'Felthams', the most advanced class of tram operated in London. Built during 1930/1931, they were still fast and strong only being redundant in London because of the closure of the Croydon services' ex-Telford Avenue Depot. Ninety were bought by Leeds at a cost, including delivery and modifications, of roughly £1,000 each (when a new car cost £12,000), although as the tramways were abandoned so precipitously not all operated. Three are visible here on 18th March, 1956 in Bishopgate Street with City Square in the background.

R.B. Parr

Plate 27: Halifax Corporation tramcars were always of a neat outline and towards the end of services presented quite a uniform picture. Of 3 ft 6 in. gauge, the routes of the tramways included winding streets coupled to fearsome gradients of 1:15 (7%) and 1:9 (11%). Electrical operations commenced in 1898, and ran until 1939 when railed vehicles were replaced by some of the most cheerfully-painted buses seen – green and orange contrasting with dour Halifax buildings. One hundred and forty-three cars were built for the system and, as it was said that nowhere was there more than 100 yards where the track did not either ascend or descend, brake systems were always up to date and well maintained as were the 39 miles of trackwork. The two photographs are specifically chosen, not only to show the landscape but the conditions routinely faced by motormen.

On 3rd April, 1938 car No. 111 prepared to climb the gradient away from Halifax (old Lancashire & Yorkshire) Railway Station. Beacon Hill provides the background. *W.A. Camwell*

Plate 28: Also in the 1930s, a snow shrouded, but still mobile, car moves almost noiselessly along Commercial Street. Trams normally ran long after pneumatic tyred vehicles had failed, but a good supply of dry sand was desirable with extra carried in an old dustbin under the stairs. *Halifax Courier*

Plate 29: Belfast once had one of the greatest tramway systems, if little known outside of Ireland. Not only was an intensive system worked, but each new batch of cars was an improvement on its predecessors (which was not always the case elsewhere), although financial constraints meant many older cars staying in service too long. 'Chamberlain' cars were introduced in 1930, were orthodox in design, although advanced electrically, and were sturdy, workmanlike cars. Sixty-six seaters, with blue leather seats, they were fast having two 50 hp motors and gave a very comfortable ride. Air brakes gave the motormen security to use the power and heaters pleased passengers in inclement weather. No. 354, a Brush product, is standing at Oldpark Terminus, while in the background can be seen the turning circle of the Cliftonville trolleybus service.
R.C. Ludgate

Plate 30: Col L. McCreary who had become General Manager of the Belfast City Tramways introduced his new streamline 4-wheel tram of the future in 1935. Twenty were built by English Electric, and to give local employment during the depression, 30 by the Service Motor Works, Belfast, albeit the latter were on Hurst Nelson of Motherwell underframes. Thirty-two feet long on an 8 ft wheelbase truck, their blue leather upholstered spring seats accommodated 64 passengers. The overhang, coupled with the weight of the controllers and other fixed gear, caused the platforms to droop slightly and the bodies to leak. As the tramways were run down, and their maintenance reduced, all bar 10 of this class were scrapped by November 1953, the simpler 'Chamberlains' lasting until the end. In June 1954, McCreary car No. 431, an English Electric car, is having the pole swung at the Springfield Road terminus of the Springfield–Ballygomartin route. This was an unusually indirect cross-city working of some 3½ miles for a ½ mile journey as a Belfast crow flies. Chamberlain cars are in the background.
R.C. Ludgate

Plate 31: BIRMINGHAM CORPORATION TRAMWAYS

When tramcars were delivered by rail, as most were, they arrived in two parts and with various items loose-packed. Assembly then took place at the depot (or in some cases out of doors or in rented property). No. 661 was photographed outside Hockley Depot in January 1924 when she was the last of her class of 25 cars to be delivered. Technically this is an odd photograph, all the more so as having blanked out other parts of the depot, brickwork can be seen through the glazing!

Some local influence can be seen in the choice of the Midland Railway Carriage & Wagon Company of Washwood Heath to build the bodies as Mr A. Baker, the BCT General Manager, always stressed the importance of using known, rather than experimental, equipment. The MRC&W Co. had never built tramcar bodies.

English Electric (ex Dick, Kerr) motors were chosen, EMB (of West Bromwich) were to supply the maximum-traction bogies, and the braking systems. Since Birmingham used narrow (3 ft 6 in.) gauge tracks, dimensions are worth noting for comparative purposes: length of saloon 21 ft 0 in., and weight ex-shops 16 tons. Fully laden with 64 seated passengers, plus standing, it was estimated that they weighed in excess of 19 tons.

Initially, to our eyes at least, the interiors were dreary with oak polished wood panelling and longitudinal wooden benches downstairs, albeit transverse (2 + 1) upstairs. Following passenger complaints, cushioned transverse seats were fitted in both saloons from 1927 onwards, reducing capacity by two. An oddity of the interior was that the ventilator glasses upstairs were of a pink glass which could do awful things to a local girl's sallow complexion! In the event the Midland Railway Carriage & Wagon Company's workmanship had proved excellent and No. 661 was not broken up until July 1953 after running 898,000 miles. *Authors' Collection*

Plate 32: On 18th March, 1939 four of the oldest cars are seen 'on shed' at Roseberry Street depot. All are from the so-called 'Radial' class built between 1906 and 1907. The bodies were from the United Electric Car Company but the trucks were of a patented design which, in theory, gave some flexibility to their movement. A problem with any 4-wheeler is that the overhang at each end cannot be reduced by lengthening the wheelbase as the 'turning circle' increases dramatically. Originally open-fronted, the platforms were vestibuled by 1930. No. 97 was withdrawn in June 1939 and No. 115 in April but Nos. 113 and 127 were reprieved by the onset of war until 1945. The general cleanliness and tidiness of this running shed was normal; the mucky state of many of today's diesel bus garages would not be tolerated. *W.A. Camwell*

Plate 33: While Rotherham's single-ended cars were built thus, Plymouth Corporation Tramways Nos. 113–127 were conversions of much older cars built for the Plymouth & Devonport Tramways Company. Absorbed with the company into the Corporation fleet, No. 118 (ex-No. 6) and her sisters underwent considerable modifications. The 'leading' end was enclosed and the staircase taken out, while at the trailing end the reversed staircase was replaced by a normal one, although curiously this entry was left open to the weather. The rear controller was left *in situ* but rarely used. Seating capacity (longitudinal downstairs) remained at 48 and they were painted in a cheerful, if unusual, yellow and white until withdrawn in 1932.

Authors' Collection

Plate 34: Shown this photograph, a transport colleague thought it was of a 1950s bus or trolleybus; in reality it was one of those rarest of beasts, a single ended tramcar. Owned by Rotherham, No. 2 was one of a class of 11 bought as long ago as 1934/5 for use on the through service to Sheffield which had loops at each end thus obviating the necessity for a forward entrance and staircase, although controllers were fitted at the 'wrong' end in the case of emergency. Seats were fixed as they would be for a motor bus and, when new, the whole image was bright and novel. Unfortunately wartime lack of maintenance made them rather dilapidated and, faced with bridge reconstruction at Tinsley, the through service ceased in 1948.

W.J. Haynes

The 8th October, 1960 was a day of infamy in tramway circles. It is true that rail and electricity costs were rising and that the tramways of Sheffield could be shown to be making a loss. But think how much was, and is, paid in subsidy to carry an ever diminishing number of omnibus passengers. Their numbers have declined, mainly because of perceived traffic congestion (it takes as long by car but *feels* longer in a bus) and because industry has virtually died in Sheffield. Industry needed trams to provide swift, comfortable and warm transport and trams needed industry to provide the passengers.

Plates 35 and 36: Two magnificent cars pass the photographer as the night closes in on 6th October, 1960. Photographs like this are how we really ought to remember traditional tramcars. They were, in Sheffield at least, always clean, were lit up like a liner that passed on a darkened sea, were warm and comfortable. They were fast on the reserved track where it was safe to hurry, with 35–40 mph easily attainable, but so very safe with air and track braking systems immediately available – an ability to stop in any weather conditions which cannot be attained by a rubber tyred vehicle. No. 258 was built by the Corporation Workshops in 1936 and No. 510, their swansong, was one of a batch of 35 built as late as 1950–52. Neither was anywhere near life-expired and it seemed quite wrong to drive the cars into the shed for the last time.

A.E. Dixon

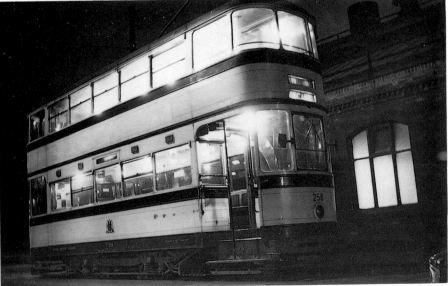

Plate 37: Some tramways may be said to have been successful from the start and for a few there was genuine regret when they were forced to close, as in the case of Sheffield, by causes beyond their control. The Leamington & Warwick had neither success nor was there regret at their closure. In fact from their very inception they suffered from a nasty taste left by their predecessors, the horse trams; they faced vehement opposition to the tracks being laid and by 1914, only nine years after the start of services, bitter complaints, not only about the trams but also the condition of the roads, poured into Leamington Council offices. The 16th August, 1930 saw the last passenger carrying tramcar to run between Leamington and Warwick.

Authors' Collection

Plate 38: Dundee Tramways was one of those concerns that presented a neat, tight, profile to visitors. The motormen and conductors alike were courteous and smart and both the cars and trackwork were well maintained. Car No. 5 began life as a bogie, double deck, open-topped, non-vestibuled 57-seater, being built by Dick, Kerr in 1900. Within 10 years all this class of 10 cars had gained roofs. In 1930 a 'paper' rebuilding took place with the shell of each body, including car No. 5, being placed on a new steel frame; new enclosed vestibules were fitted, seating (cushioned) was increased to 66, and more importantly, a new 4-wheel truck was fitted powered by 2×50 hp motors. Air brakes and magnetic track brakes replaced the old hand brake.

Thus rejuvenated No. 5 lasted until the end of 1955, some parts of her bodywork being no less than 55 years old – a testimony to seasoned wood. The photograph is dated 5th August, 1955 and the location is West Port Junction, N. Tay Street leading off to the right and S. Tay Street to the left. The last Dundee tram ran on Thursday 25th October, 1956.

H.B. Priestley

Plate 39: The lettering 'Great Grimsby Street Tramways Co.' was always puzzling to a young postcard collector as it seemed very grandiose to use 'Great' in a title and how could a tramway not be a street tramway? That the trams also ran from the People's Park to Cleethorpes made them almost foreign. Opened on 7th December, 1901, the lines were taken over from the Provincial Tramways Group by Grimsby Corporation in 1925 and were closed on 17th July, 1937. Car No. 59 was one of three home-built by the Great Grimsby Street Tramways Company in 1927, albeit utilising components from older cars, but it says much for the ingenuity of the staff of such a small concern that they could undertake and finish the work in a satisfactory manner. *Authors' Collection*

Plate 40: Weston-super-Mare Tramways offered virtually all that a seaside tramway could to visitors and locals alike. It would have been better had the proposed connection from the Weston, Clevedon and Portishead Light Railway to Locking Road been completed, or even better had one been able to take the through train from Weston to Portishead. Probably taken in the early 1930s, this photograph shows two typical Weston-super-Mare cars in Knightstone Road, with No. 18, the so-called toastrack nearer, one of a type loved by holidaymakers. Delivered in 1927 with seats for 52, local people claim 100 passengers were regularly carried. The open top double decker, No. 6, is unusual inasmuch as it is carrying no advertisements, although enamel plates advertised the 'Grove Park Grill' until 1930. No. 6 was one of the original batch built by Brush in 1902. Weston-super-Mare Tramways closed on 17th April, 1937 in favour of Bristol Tramways' buses. Primarily this was due to the length of single track joined by passing loops which so slowed the cars' operation that, towards the end, the average speed rarely exceeded 5 mph for the entire journey from Sanatorium to Old Pier. *A.E. Dixon*

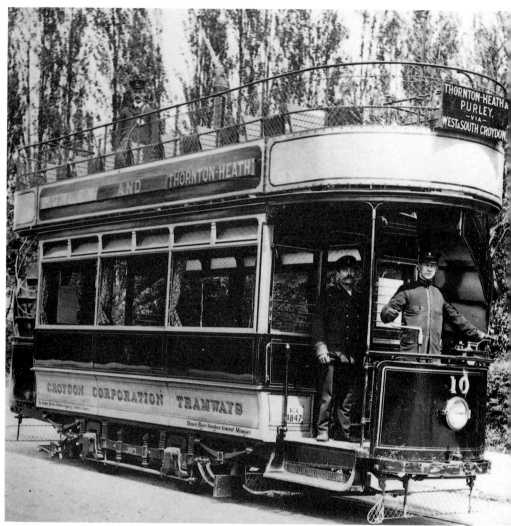

Plate 41: One of the accusations made against London tramcars was that they were all alike. This was true towards the end of services, by which time it was sensible from a maintenance angle to keep only a handful of designs at work, but, in earlier days, the London Transport Passenger Board inherited a plethora of shapes and sizes from their predecessors, the LCC, the local councils and private companies. Although No. 10 is lettered as a Croydon Corporation car, between 1901 and 1905 she was operated by a subsidiary of the British Electric Traction Company, Croydon & District Tramways.

The photograph shows a simple, almost basic, tramcar with reversed stairs, a canopy over the driver, four wheel truck and very primitive lifeguard. Built at a cost of £650 by the oldest company in the tramcar building list, G.F. Milnes & Co. of Hadley, in 1901 she was one of a class totalling 35. A pure traditional car, No. 10 measured 28 ft long, 6 ft 2 in. wide, stood 9 ft 11 in. tall and weighed 7½ tons unladen. As an indication of the space lost by having two platforms for the driver and the double-ended passenger loading arrangement, the saloon was only 16 ft long, i.e. four-sevenths only of the vehicle. Longitudinal seats downstairs seated 11 a side, but floral curtains cheered up the dark polished wood. The ventilator glasses were a 'golden' yellow, and upstairs, with seats for 30, water-proof cotton covers were provided for use in the rain. The reversed stairs, said to be safe for passengers, totally obscured the driver's vision on his left.

The uniforms, not dissimilar to a Japanese Naval Petty Officer's were short-lived with the more usual 'railway pattern' appearing before 1910. The lifeguards are of the Wilson & Bennett mesh type, which, on striking an obstruction, caused the underfloor tray to drop. Experiments showed that at above 12 mph they were of little use, the motor banging against the obstruction while the tray was still falling. No. 10 was scrapped in 1927.

Authors' Collection

Plate 42: No. 4 of the South Metropolitan Electric Tramways Company's fleet was built by Brush in 1906 with a semi-flexible truck built under Lycett & Conaty patents. She is shown as refitted in the 1920s with Warner radial gear. The slightly longer saloons of this class of 16 cars – 19 ft 9 in. out of a total length of 31 ft 10 in. – allowed for 28 seats inside but the narrow bodies (6 ft) restricted the 'outside' to 30. Two noticeable differences compared with No. 10 are the stairs which were of the 'normal' pattern, and at each end of the car are steel hoops named after their inventor. Experience showed that just occasionally a trolley mast, the spring or even a pole itself could break and the passengers underneath were put in real hazard; a difficulty obviated by the use of Spencer hoops as these deflected this errant material to one side. There were also recorded occasions during the World War I blackout when passengers standing up or taking their seats on ordinary cars were struck by the trolley pole as it was swung around.

SMET No. 4 survived long enough in London Transport days to be re-numbered 4S and was allocated the serial number 3484, but was scrapped in 1935. The enamel coated cast-iron advertisements would be worth a fortune now and were fine examples of the art.

Authors' Collection

Plate 43: We do not know exactly why this photograph was taken, although it is assumed it was in connection with roadworks. The picture is looking from Mare Street, Hackney, towards the Mare Street 'Triangle' near its junction with Lower Clapton Road and it is recorded that it was taken at 10.30 am on Tuesday 13th December, 1938. We also know that here is a truly beautiful London tramscape: conduit working leaving a skyline uncluttered by wires, superbly maintained track and road surface are evident and departing is a 'typical' London tram. Route 31 which once ran to Battersea 'Princes Head' from Hackney had, by 1939, been cut back to Wandsworth via Shoreditch, Clerkenwell Road, Bloomsbury, Kingsway Subway, Westminster & Vauxhall, but still a pleasant 72 minute journey and with a car every 8–10 minutes you did not have long to wait!

Authors' Collection

Plate 44: The Croydon Corporation Tramways' line from High Street, South Croydon to Addiscombe was abandoned as early as 28th March, 1927 and replaced by a new London General Omnibus Company service 178. It is said that, towards the end, the trackwork was fairly awful as the concrete foundations had collapsed and allowed the rails to undulate. Basically this was due to neglect during World War I and, having ascertained that the 68 tramwaymen directly affected would be offered alternative transport by the LGOC, one feels the Corporation were pleased enough to wash their hands of the whole affair. But what a scene we have here: this is Lower Addiscombe Road and the pub is the Leslie Arms; despite the ˙rocious weather a hardy passenger sits outside, but the saloon looks fuggy and happily crowded. Everyone stops for the photographer as the rain ˙es down: truly a microcosm of tramway life in its heyday.

Authors' Collection

Plate 45: South Metropolitan Electric Tramways had rather a rag-bag of cars bequeathed to them by the British Electric Traction Company and, being very non-standard, only a handful survived to see service with London Transport.

29 was transferred to SMET in 1906 having previously served in Croydon. Very large trams, being 34 ft 8 in. overall, the saloon, however, was a mere 22 ft long, albeit seating 30. Two bogies carried ten tons of weight, and with only a total of 50 hp available, they were slow cars. The use of the safety double-flight staircases and wide entry doors made them remarkably easy for the passenger to use. The denting of the front panels first appeared in a photograph of 1925, and car bearing the same scars went for scrap nine years later.   *London Transport*

Plate 46: At the same location, and photographed within a few days of No. 29 (but a radically different car), No. 34 was of type 'O' within the South Metropolitan Electric Tramways Company's fleet. She was built in 1902 for the Gravesend and Northfleet Tramway Company's service but sold to SMET in 1906 for £560. Fitted with two bogie trucks No. 34 had the so-called 'reversed' stairs, generally held to be safer as passengers could not fall out of the car, but which left the driver completely blind on his left hand side. Stored in 1931, No. 34 had the dubious honour of being the last to be broken up in June 1934. In their day, though, they were a usefully large vehicle, seating 68 and with two 30 hp motors were a little faster than many other SMET cars. No. 34 was unique in one respect in that she retained her wire-mesh, rather than slatted, 'dog guards' between the bogies, which were added by SMET under pressure from the Board of Trade Inspectors. They were, one supposes, unlikely to be worried about dogs but when trams were waiting at the terminus small children had a penchant for playing tag through the gap. The provision of 'dog guards' ensured instead that the children climbed up the outside of the staircase to get upstairs!   *London Transport*

Plates 47 and 48: Unusually these are two photographs of the same car, the first taken just prior to repainting in 'state', rather than 'Company', colours. The Metropolitan Electric Tramways Company was the largest of the private companies which operated in London, with 53.74 route miles under their control although most were leased to them by local councils. No. 2309 (former 141) was one of only 15 single deck cars, all alike, owned by the company and used on services to Alexandra Palace. The route closed on 23rd February, 1938 and the cars were immediately scrapped. Both photographs are posed. 'Don't tramp it, tram it' (seen on No. 141) was a famous slogan while the infamous bleak Inspectors' huts were equally well known. *MET Photo (top) London Transport (below)*

Plate 49: The reader will have noted by now that these London cars abounded in variety and it was a source of aggravation to many small boys that their stencil, or blind, boxes for the route numbers almost invariably occupied part, or most, of the front upper deck window. To our minds this was a very bad design! Exactly why these boxes were varied. Nos. 2238, 552 and 565 and the other two cars in this picture, all have different permutations of indicators, 2238 adding to the problems by having a rattling blind which has wound itself back to halfway between Holborn and Waltham Cross. No. 2238 was an ex-Metropolitan Electric Tramways Company type 'H', built 1911 and scrapped 1938, the arched saloon windows being quite distinctive. Nos. 552 and 565 were in class 'E/1', the nearest the London County Council had to a standard tram, but had electrical equipment frugally recovered from the famous Kingsway Subway single deckers and were known as 'Reconstructed Subway Cars'. Built in 1930, they led uneventful lives until premature destruction in 1951/2. *W.A. Camwell*

Plate 50: Car No. 1142 of the London County Council's fleet is seen at Thornton Heath. Route 16 was an interesting service from Purley to The Embankment via Croydon, Thornton Heath, Norbury, Streatham, Brixton, Kennington, Westminster, Blackfriars, Elephant & Castle, Kennington and so back to Purley. To balance this one-way circle route 18 did the same in reverse and to add to the vehicular interest the LCC & Croydon Corporation ran both routes as a joint service. Hurst Nelson of Motherwell had a reputation for good workmanship but also from the 1920s on they suffered from hardening of the tramway arteries. No. 1142 was one of an order for 175 identical cars delivered during 1908/9 and which was followed by orders for nearly 900 others. Thereafter it was said that even in the 1950s Hurst Nelson still quoted for variations of this class believing there was none better. Dimensions were to LCC 'Standard': 78 seats, 33 ft 10 in. long overall, 7 ft 2 in. wide, 15 ft 9¾ in. from railhead to trolley plank, 2 × 25 hp motors. *Authors' Collection*

Plate 51: This Metropolitan Electric Tramways' car (former No. 62) was a rare survivor into London Transport days and is seen here on special duty at Hendon for RAF Day in 1934. Many of this class had been fitted with enclosed tops but No. 2515 soldiered on in her original state, wooden seats included. She was scrapped in 1936. The triangle was (and on the continent still is) a warning of powerful air brakes.

Authors' Collection

Plate 52: An unusual photograph inasmuch as it was taken during the war at Abbey Wood, South London. This was unusual on two accounts. Photography was difficult as, although not prohibited, various officials could and would be obstructive, quoting the Defence of the Realm Act for their actions. Obtaining film was another problem. The blast netting on the windows is to reduce the risk of flying splinters but the oblongs and lozenges were to enable passenger to see where they were. White-painted bumpers aided people's vision at night, as did the rings on the poles. Masked headlights added to pedestrians' hazards but reduced the risk of being seen by enemy aircraft. Car No. 295 was a one-off, the first totally enclosed tram to be built at West Ham Corporation's Greengate Street Works and the last car to be built there, this happening in 1931. No. 295 (West Ham 68) was transferred to Abbey Wood in June 1940 and scrapped in July 1952.

W.J. Haynes

Plate 53: No. 544, wearing all the typical accoutrements of a London tramcar – side destination and '1/– all day every day' boards, Oxo and holiday advertisements – is seen on route 5 Moorgate–Hampstead, which in 1933 had a 4–5 minute service headway and a single fare end-to-end of 4*d*. – return 6*d*. This tram route ended in July 1938 being replaced by trolleybus service 639, and this 1906 car was scrapped a year later. *W.A. Camwell*

Plate 54: Route 72 which ran from Savoy Street, Strand to Woolwich was one of the most interesting of the conduit routes, including New Cross and Shooters Hill in its itinerary. The journey time in the mid-1930s was 70 minutes and the fare 5*d*. The '72' was one of the last routes to be closed in London, when the tragic death knell of a magnificent fleet was heard and seen. Everywhere posters told us it was the 'Last tram week – On the 5th of July [1952] we say goodbye to London'. Car No. 169 was originally owned by Leyton Council although built to LCC design. *Authors' Collection*

The story of Blackpool's tramways has been well documented, not the least in Steve Palmer and Philip Higgs' *Trams to the Tower*, which is not only readable but extraordinarily well illustrated. The two photographs which follow are therefore only intended to demonstrate two widely separated aspects of tram car operation in a seaside town.

Plate 55: The reverse of this card asks 'How do you like Albert and his pleasant look: doesn't he look married?', and the writer signs 'Clare' with two kisses. Which is Albert? We shall never know, for this is Blackpool and the photograph one of many thousands taken by a Mr Wiggins who waited near the Oxford Hotel, Marton, and captured the expressions of each band of happy trippers on the famous Marton Circular Tour. Twenty-two of these toastracks existed, built between 1911 and 1914, seating 69 until 1936–7 when, to reduce the accidents to conductors who necessarily climbed around the outside when the car was in motion, they were converted to centre aisle, leaving 55 usable seats.

Authors' Collection

Plate 56: This car represents one of the great near-misses that have bedevilled British tramway history. On paper the 25 cars of the 'Coronation' class, built by Charles Roberts of Wakefield and delivered between 1952 and 1954, should have been world-beaters, for with fluorescent lighting, a glass panelled roof to ensure a light interior, remotely controlled sliding doors and luxurious seating for 56 passengers (then a high number for a comfortable single decker) with reasonable legroom, there was nothing to equal them. But they did not have one Achilles heel but a number. They rusted. They leaked. Due to the complicated nature of their control system, designed to give a better ride and faster acceleration, they were both unreliable and extremely heavy on power consumption, roughly double that of a standard car. Built at a cost of £12,000 each (six times that of a motor-bus) the first was scrapped in 1968 after an unbelievably short life. Fortuitously the car shown, No. 304, has been preserved in more or less original condition.

Authors' Collection

Plate 57: The saddest part of the story of the Swansea and Mumbles Tramway is not so much its going, but how nearly one of the magnificent 106 seater cars might have been saved after the line's closure on 5th January, 1960. It was rescued and stored where it should have been safe but the vandals arrived and that was the end. Generally said to have been the oldest passenger carrying railway in the world – like the Oystermouth Railway (actually a plateway) it dated back to 1807 – it was electrified in 1928 when the cars of this design were built by Brush. Earlier traction attempts had included four Hughes enclosed steam tram engines in 1877, three battery-electric cars in 1902/3 and between five and seven orthodox steam engines from 1892. The photograph was taken on 17th September, 1959.   A.E. Dixon

Plates 58 and 59: These two photographs have been selected to show a couple of the idiosyncracies of the Hill of Howth Transport. There were others, as for example it was one of only a handful owned by a main-line railway – the Great Northern Railway. Five and five-eighths miles long, it used the wide gauge of 5 ft 3 in. Two of the ten cars, most of which dated back to 1901, remained to the end, painted in Mr Gresley's favourite teak finish, commonly found on elderly stock wandering around East Anglia, even in the late 1950s. The others were in a beautiful blue and cream livery. The line closed on 31st May, 1959, being no longer fashionable. Howth summit is 407 ft above sea-level.

The tramway's greatest oddity was these traffic lights at Howth single line section installed because the other end of the line is out of sight. The light aspect when lit indicated 'line clear' but when out indicated the line was occupied although, of course, it was a fail-safe in the event of bulb or electricity failure. The second photograph shows an oblique overbridge which carried the tramway over another tramway, the Clontarf and Hill of Howth, which ran from Howth Harbour to Dollymount. Both pictures were taken on 31st May, 1959.   R.C. Ludgate

Between 1880 and 1930 there appeared a number of 'Do-it-Yourself' instruction books for use by a would-be tramway engineer. There was also a tram drivers' handbook which unfortunately pre-supposed a higher level of literacy than was to be found prior to World War I; the very nature of the work and the hours worked by drivers left them little time to improve their education. In fairness though, it has to be said that those who tried to gain knowledge were normally rewarded with a better position.

Plate 60: Basic circuitry is interesting; the main difficulty, if one is not to have excessive current consumption, is that the continuity between the overhead conductor via the trolley wheel or skate through the wheels to the track must be good. Initially it was poor, due partially to a lack of understanding of the forces involved and to the physical condition of rail heads set in roads normally used by horse-drawn vehicles. Later as neglect took its toll, the overhead became worn with locked trolleywheels not unknown, while rail imperfections and loss of bonding led to a bad return.

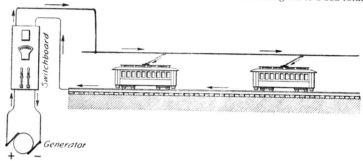

Plate 61 (bottom right): This shows a power feed to the overhead, and the insulated junction between two sections. The live wires are normally carried over the line of the track and have to be at a minimum of 17 ft above the road surface, although 20 ft was more usual in towns and cities. Obviously the further the vehicle was from its main power source then the less the available electricity and the slower it would go. This, too, is governed by legal requirements placed upon the tramway operators. The first is that the voltage must not exceed 600 with the current automatically cut off if there is an overload. Secondly, whatever the voltage chosen the drop between one end of a section and another must not exceed 7 volts. Finally sections must not be more than ½ mile long. Although not visible in the photograph, a section box (often a featureless oblong on the pavement used mostly by dogs to lean on) will normally be adjacent to the pole carrying the feeder.

The section insulators dividing up the overhead into independent lengths are clearly visible; the click-click heard as a trolley wheel passed over these was one of the sounds most missed by people whose houses were adjacent to tram-tracks.

Authors' Collection

Plate 62 (below left): Rail bonding not only ensures good continuity of current but is a legal require-ment. As anyone who has ever fiddled with any electrical apparatus (whether mains or battery) knows, electrical current takes the shortest route to earth – a nice nearby iron, water, or gas, pipe represents a far easier route for stray electricity to return back to its source (i.e. the generator) than the relatively high resistance of steel rails. Lead sheathed telephone cables in ducts are better still. Introduce electricity to iron and corrosion is immediate (consider the earthing points on cars as a comparison) and although telephone cables normally carry 50.5 volts, 600 v causes, at very least, severe interference. Fishplates – mechanical joints – offer poor continuity primarily as they wear loose and the actual area of contact can be pathetically small, so a heavy copper wire bypass is required. If good earthing bonds are used the actual loss of electricity should be limited to 2 amperes per mile of track or about 5 per cent of the available current.

Authors' Collection

Plate 62

Plate 61

The causes of wear to trackwork are manifold. A catalogue of the 1920s shows 140 different sections, all purporting to wear more evenly, to be of superior materials or to give better continuity. There were (and are) relevant British Standards, with certain dimensions governed by law. For example, as laid the groove must not exceed 1⅛ in. in width on the straight and 1¼ in. on a curve.

Tramway rails have, normally, flat level treads when new which eventually become convex, while wheel tyres, initially level, wear concave.

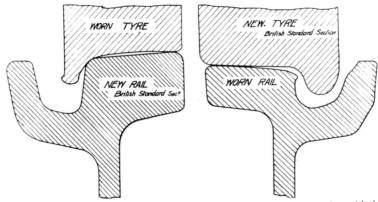

Plate 63: Shows the result quite clearly, the worn tyre has only pinpoint connection with the rail and will wear quickly not only on the bearing face but on the flange. Clearly the gauge between the flanges is then greater than it should be, and the resultant clatter, even on plain rail will accelerate this wear. Conversely a new tyre on worn rail will quite surprisingly quickly take the profile of a worn rail while simultaneously grinding away at new rail where this meets the old.

Plate 64: Shows how far out of gauge the rails can go — in this case it was 4 ft 9¾ in. rather than 4 ft 8½ in. The way in which the worn rail has almost melted, or at least been squashed into forming a lip inside the groove is noteworthy. The head also gives the impression of having been displaced where it meets the shoulder. *Authors' Collection*

Plate 65: A stack of new rails awaiting laying, showing the profile as laid. *Authors' Collection*

A traditional tramway is, in effect, a street railway using on the public highway a grooved or slotted rail which guides the steel tyres of the wheels. On reserved or private trackwork this groove is unnecessary and ordinary rail can be utilised. Problems immediately arise when you put two, four or more grooves down the middle of the road. Cycle tyres enter them, car tyre treads can be damaged, small children put stones (and worse) in them. Sand blows along and rapidly ensures the road surface is smooth, while the horse did his best to hide all traces of trackwork. Rails expand and contract in the weather and unless foundation work is watched will move, tie bars and retaining ironwork notwithstanding. There was a spot where the trackwork had so shifted on a curve that the tramcar's rear bogie invariably rumbled along the cobbles for a couple of yards before regaining its rightful place. Subsidence also could occur, Pontypridd at one time having its rails 12 inches or more above the road, as the road fell away.

Most tram tracks are laid on a concrete foundation over well rammed stone, preferably granite chippings not exceeding ¾ in. diameter. Scientifically mass concrete takes ten years to finish curing, tram tracks often had less than 5 hours. For example, one night in Sheffield a 400 yard length was relaid. At 6 am a steamroller and load of steel crossed left to right. Even at 5 mph we rolled and twisted our way across the depression he created. The Inspector was summoned and cars were thereafter 'walked' across until the whole job could be done again.

Plate 66 (top left): A dropped rail joint or fractured rail was said to be the cause of this Aberdeen car 'taking to the fields'.
The Omnibus Society

Plate 67 (top right): Lowestoft. The condition of the tracks is all too visible. Authors' Collection

Plate 68 (bottom left): Worn and twisted trackwork on a curve. The scoring of the adjacent tarmac shows the route the cars preferred. Authors' Collection

Plate 69 (bottom right): A pre-World War I photograph showing the appalling wear on both cobbles and railhead caused by the iron tyres of solid unsprung wheels in an industrial city. The carters preferred to use the rail to gain a smoother ride. Repairs were paid for from the tramways' own funds, and not by the Highway Authorities. Authors' Collection

Plate 70: A view of the loop at Fleetwood shortly before relaying showing how patching of the road surface can only ameliorate its condition once the rails have begun to move, whether in a vertical or horizontal plane.

Authors' Collection

Four photographs without a tram in sight. Despite agreements by tramway companies to obviate or reduce problems during the period of track laying, life for the townsfolk became fraught with problems. Shops neared bankruptcy as people and delivery vans alike stayed away while dirt and dust was everywhere. Three of the photographs also show three different forms of electrical power transmission.

Plate 71: To avoid 'unsightly' overhead wires and the necessary poles or standards which supported them, Torquay adopted the Dolter stud contact whereby power was transmitted to the cars by means of a skate rubbing on live brass plates or studs, themselves made live by the passage of the car. Opened in 1907, stud contact was not a success and was replaced by overhead equipment during 1911, the system closing in 1934.

The pots which carried the studs can clearly be seen – not the least of the problems incurred by any of these underground systems was that unless workmanship was of the highest quality electrical joints could fail and unlike similar faults in overhead wiring, which is accessible, repairs were a major operation. Quite often due to grit and horse-muck jamming its innards a contact would stick in the 'live' position. As it carried a nominal 550 volts a warning bell notified the conductor that he had to nail a piece of asbestos over the unit before the car could proceed. Then a gang of men (known as the 'Dolter Murderers'!) would attend to it. Photograph taken at the junction of Newton Road/Upton Road and Higher Union Street in Torquay. Trade to the 'Motor Garage', who advertised as 'General Engineers and Smiths' and 'Motor Cars Supplied', must have been totally lost during the conversion.

Local History Collection, Torquay Public Library

Plate.72: A 1898 photograph, this shows the laying of expensive conduit trackwork at Wandsworth Road station. London was the only British town or city to persevere with this method of current collection, had a plough shaped contact bar which picked up the current from a live cable in a trough. This illustration depicts a junction and the complications are obvious, but as a method of working, given good maintenance, it was an excellent way of reducing opposition to overhead wires. Served by routes 26 and 28 in London County Council days, 30 to 35 trams passed here every hour.

Authors' Collection

Plate 73: This is Worcester in 1904; standards and wires are in place and the track laying is underway. This scene was described by local historians as the 'Worcester electric tramway seige' and the protracted works contributed to the tramway's unpopularity and eventual closure as early as 1928.

A British Electric Traction Company tramway, like Torquay narrow (3 ft 6 in.) gauge was adopted. Despite this complaints of traffic jams began almost as soon as the tramway opened and it is significant that as soon as Worcester Corporation took over the network the trams were replaced by buses of the Birmingham & Midland Motor Omnibus Company Ltd (Midland Red) who rapidly gained a monopoly.

Authors' Collection

Plate 74 (opposite): In the heyday of both tramways and railways there were a number of steelworks who specialised in the provision of 'special' trackwork. On plain, level track wear is more-or-less constant but as soon as curves, points (turnouts) and, to a lesser extent, stopping places are introduced certain parts of the rail will wear – often quite dramatically. There were various ways to overcome this – water fountains which provided lubrication on a curve for example – but in general the practice was to replace certain parts of the rail with hardened or toughened insert.

One such specialist is Edgar Allen Ltd of Sheffield, whose connection with tramway track certainly dates back to 1883 if not earlier. Manganese steel was first introduced in 1901 and, except for cost, could well have replaced crucible cast steel in any pointwork. A quote from 1928: 'Economically – the advantage of Manganese Steel lies in the greatly increased life, which is now well known. This advantage, connected with the cost of earlier changes and renewals, makes it without doubt, THE material for Track Work, and more than compensates for the increased first cost. It is too hard to be machined and therefore has to be ground. It is so tough that it may be bent double when cold without fracture. Its resistance to abrasion is phenomenal, and it is also non-magnetic.'

One beautiful piece of 'special work' was this fan of 27 tracks for use at Kirkstall Road Depot, Leeds, seen here assembled at the works. Holts' Rolled Manganese guard rail was used throughout on the ner curves and all other pointwork (shown in light colour) was cast in manganese. Kirkstall Road ased to be a running shed in 1931, with the rather eccentric result that Leeds Corporation Tramways d a repair and maintenance works with a storage capacity of nearly half the operational fleet! This was to last until the closure of Kirkstall Road in November 1957. *Edgar Allan Engineering*

Plate 75: Swadlincote depot of the Burton & Ashby Light Railway in 1915. The building on the right was the power station where electricity was generated, surprisingly not by coal as was usual at the time, but by heavy oil engines. Although a tramway insofar as orthodox Brush-built tramcars were used, the Burton & Ashby was nearer to an American pattern interurban concern, some ten miles in length. The colours reflected the Light Railway part of the title, being a glorious mixture of Midland Railway crimson lake, pure white with clear gold lining and, to break the line of the rocker panel, the Midland Railway coat-of-arms handpainted in the centre. Of narrow (3 ft 6 in.) gauge, the line opened on 13th June, 1906 and closed on 19th February, 1927.

British Railways

Plate 76 (opposite): This photograph was taken on 4th September, 1906 and shows the Aberhill shed or 'car barn' of the Wemyss & District Tramways Company. The overhead linesmen's vehicles would hardly meet today's Health & Safety requirements! A 3 ft 6 in. gauge system, the company was a subsidiary of the Balfour Beatty combine, and one of the relatively few tramways engineered by Bruce Peebles. It was 7½ miles long and largely financed by the Wemyss Colliery Company, using private land for much of its route from Gallatown to Leven via Wemyss and Methil.

Services were interworked with Kirkaldy Corporation, cars running through to that town. The Wemyss tramways were purchased by the Scottish Motor Traction Company in March 1930 and

NEI Peebles

Without a reliable means of controlling the input of electricity to a tramcar's motors awful things could happen and indeed some very early controllers had a very short life as little account was paid to sparks etching brass fingers, and the possibility of flashovers. One must not forget too that many motormen were poorly trained and tended to ignore intermediate notches, instead trying to engage full power from a standing start.

The vastly simplified cutaway drawing shows the inside of a BTH K2 controller, but most were of similar pattern. Of the so-called '9 notch' design it was designed for two motors of up to 40 hp. It was (barely) adequate until the high power cars of the 1930s.

(1) Handle operates controller (2)

(3) Operates the reverse controller (4)

(9) Are the power 'fingers' which allow the motorman to 'notch up'. These are separated by: (5) Insulated partitions

(6) Is the protecting blow-out magnet

(7) Are quite essential being the two 'cut out' switches which enable a defective motor to be cut out of circuit, and which, incidentally, many motormen would not touch preferring to carry on regardless!

(8) Is the wiring connection or distribution board

(12) Is the 'can' or cover.

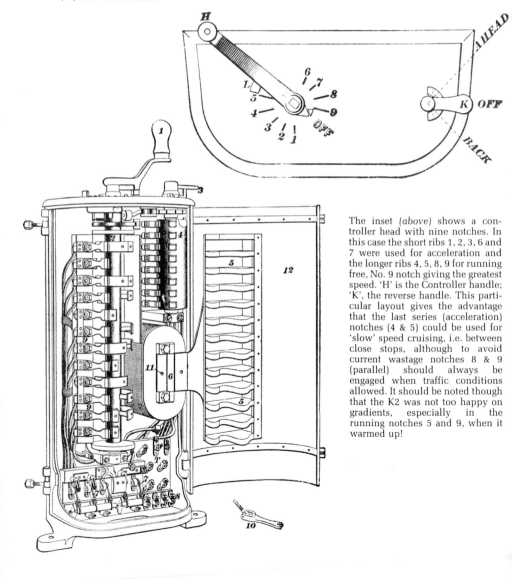

The inset *(above)* shows a controller head with nine notches. In this case the short ribs 1, 2, 3, 6 and 7 were used for acceleration and the longer ribs 4, 5, 8, 9 for running free, No. 9 notch giving the greatest speed. 'H' is the Controller handle; 'K', the reverse handle. This particular layout gives the advantage that the last series (acceleration) notches (4 & 5) could be used for 'slow' speed cruising, i.e. between close stops, although to avoid current wastage notches 8 & 9 (parallel) should always be engaged when traffic conditions allowed. It should be noted though that the K2 was not too happy on gradients, especially in the running notches 5 and 9, when it warmed up!

Plate 78: Shows a Bruce Peebles controller installed in a Wemyss Tramway car and with the spark shield open for inspection. Nine power and seven brake notches were provided, the main drum or controller when turned moved through gearing, the small drum at the side, and established the proper connections for running and braking. The blow out magnet is on the left and the isolating switches are above the 'disboard' on the right.

NEI-Peebles

In very early days there were a number of accidents involving both passers-by and passengers who got under the wheels of tramcars; even in later days it was quite heart stopping when small children ran out in the road unaware of a tramcar bearing down on them, the clatter of a life-guard falling adding to the pulse rate. Various designs have always existed but the Board of Trade (later Ministry of Transport) Inspectors quickly made their requirements known. In general most photographs show the Hudson & Bowing pattern life guard which is operated by a 'trigger', normally 2 or 3 slats as shown on car No. 220. Knocking this drops the tray (beneath the step) which scoops up the person or animal concerned.

Plate 79: Newcastle car No. 220 built by Brush in 1914. This illustration is included to show not only the lifeguard but some of the detail of these workaday and often maligned vehicles. The finish and paintwork is quite remarkable for what was an industrial and dirty city. The spring fender is particularly noteworthy.
H.O. Thompson

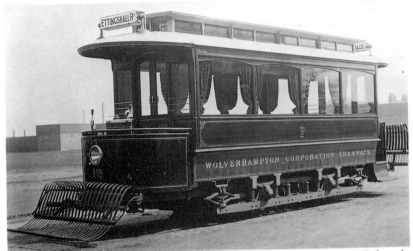

Plate 80: When Wolverhampton decided on the electric tramway its fastidious City Fathers decided against the normal overhead equipment, and instead selected the Brown surface contact system as re-designed and supplied by the Lorain Steel Company of Ohio USA. Each car carried a heavy skate 12 ft long, and weighing with its equipment over a ton, which by magnets energised a switch inside the stud and allowed power to flow to the car. It worked, but perhaps more due to the determination of the Wolverhampton Corporation Tramways Department than anything wonderful about the system. Car No. 12 was itself one of a class of oddities. Built by Milnes and mounted on Lorain DuPont trucks they could only carry 26 seated passengers and one wonders just who they were designed for. The 'Providence' lifeguards seen here were supplied with the cars in February 1902, but rapidly replaced by orthodox Wilson Bennett wire mesh type in July. The system was converted to overhead in 1921 but abandonment commenced three years later, and by November 1928 the trams were gone.

Authors' Collection

Plate 81: The Manx Electric Railway has suffered some mixed fortunes since part of this narrow gauge (3 ft) line was first opened in 1893, but it still forms a vital cog in the Manx economy. The powered tramcars are fascinating and represent the latest ideas in American street car design, albeit of a hundred years ago. The fender is more a cow-catcher and no dog-guard is fitted between the bogies. Car No. 6 was built in 1894, the open trailer, No. 41, was a replacement for a car accidentally burned at Laxey Depot in 1930.

Authors' Collection

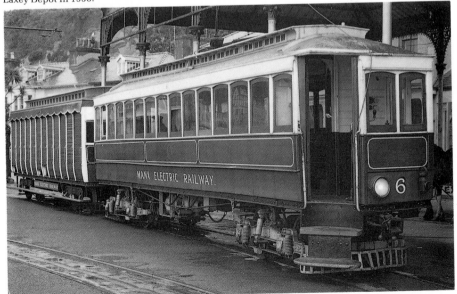

Plate 82: When tramcars go into the works quite unfriendly things are done to them and they are often left in a dishevelled state for long periods. Some never emerge but class 'E/1' No. 1584 of the London County Council fleet built by Brush in 1911, seen here at the Central Car Repair Works, Charlton, in February 1932, re-entered service by April and, hardly changed, remained in service until 1951.

Authors' Collection

Plate 83: Halifax car No. 65 on the other hand, seen here quite indecently exposed early in the 1930s, was in the workshops for some months while repairs were carried out to her framing and the platforms. New glazing, panelling and seats prolonged her life until 1938. The height and length of these cars made their 3 ft 6 in. gauge trucks seem quite out of balance.

Authors' Collection

To 'Traffic' staff maintenance men always seemed to have the mucky end of the job and, while one or two might become vaguely familiar, it was rare that a driver really came into contact with these men for they led a nocturnal kind of life.

Plate 84: The Mexborough & Swinton Tramways Company started with trams, tried trolleybuses and ended up with motorbuses. As a tram operator they had no chance of survival being saddled with the Dolter surface contact system, subsidence and low railway bridges. Curiously, the cars were dual-fitted, having a normal trolley for use in Rotherham. Services started on 3rd August, 1906 and by 1908 the Dolter was no more, but stud contact had wasted £14,000. The staff in the photograph do not appear too worried; the Manager Mr P. Priestley looks quietly confident.   *Authors' Collection*

Plate 85: Kirkaldy Corporation Tramways started business in 1904 with just over six miles of narrow gauge track. They made an end-on connection with Wemyss Tramways at Gallatown and a curiosity of the through working was that two of the Wemyss single deck cars were always stabled overnight at the Kirkaldy Depot. Twenty-six cars were used and it is interesting to note here both the variety in advertisements and that the later cars had improved all-round vision for the driver. Was the man in full driver's uniform a ferry-man used in the shed? Or was he sick or grounded for a disciplinary reason? Even in the 1950s the theoretical punishment for 'coming off the wires' was a fortnight in the works; in 1922 (when this photograph was taken) it was instant dismissal!   *Authors' Collection*

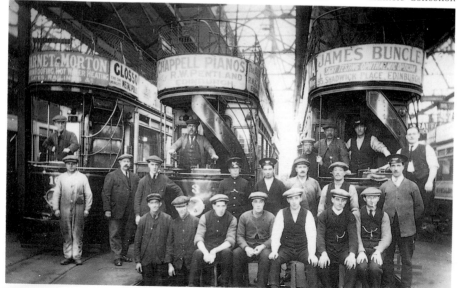

Plate 86: Where, why or when this photograph was taken is uncertain, but presumably it was a demonstration. Was the idea that one swept the 'second' set of rails or was it an early attempt to mechanise road-sweeping? The use of tramcar mounted rotary brushes of this pattern, chain or gear driven, was normal until the end of horse traffic, but rarely used offset as shown. The offensive sludge that coated roads, particularly in cities, beggared description and nocturnal sorties with a sweeper were absolutely essential. The main problem was, of course, that the muck was only displaced and got squeezed back onto the tracks. Such a brush could also be used as a snow broom although on one occasion the snow melted slightly and was clearing well when the crew went for a cup of tea. On return it had frozen again with each bristle of the brush a mini-icicle. The racket was dreadful and after a few hundred yards the car swizzled to a stop, having to be pushed back to the shed. Explanations were difficult.   *Authors' Collection*

Plate 87: Taken a few years ago, this picture shows OMO Car 11 at Blackpool's Rugby Road Depot. OMO 11 was once a beautiful English Electric rail coach, No. 615, and was modified in 1975, using part of a grant from the Ministry of Transport. The grants were designed to eliminate conductors from all passenger carrying vehicles, whether rubber- or steel-tyred. That they also increased unemployment by thousands was irrelevant.   *Authors' Collection*

Cars of the 1930s In the 1920s and early 1930s various tramway committees still foresaw a reasonably long life for their tramways and track relaying was carried out to quite an extensive degree. Originally the tramways had been purchased or built on borrowed money and, this generally being due for final payment in the 1940s, their reasoning was not entirely altruistic. A surprising number also experimented with building modern-outline rolling stock, although in 'penny packets'.

Plate 88: Huddersfield ordered six of these cars in 1930, English Electric supplying them a year later. Four-wheelers, they seated 62 passengers and were powered by 2 × 50 hp motors on an 8 ft wheelbase truck. The comparison with older, open balcony cars of the type shown in the background of this photograph taken at Longroyd Bridge Depot in 1938 was marked and made the clientele dissatisfied with the existing vehicles. Nos. 137–144 were sold to Sunderland in 1938 when the rails on the Long Marsden route were lifted.   *W.A. Camwell*

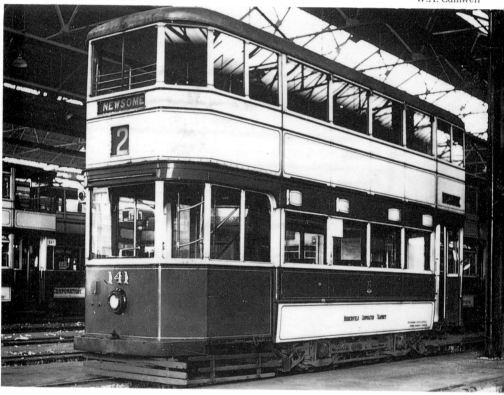

Plate 89 (opposite, top): Arthur R. Fearnley General Manager of Sheffield Corporation Tramways was far-sighted enough to see that some tram routes were not worth their cost, and could be abandoned. With the money saved, and with a little cajoling of the Transport Committee, new cars which would increase patronage could be introduced on a rolling programme. No. 207 was one of the famous 'Sheffield Standards' and was built in 1935 as one of a class of 210. With 61 upholstered seats and 2 × 50 hp motors, they were both fast and sweet riding. A.R. Fearnley retired in 1936 after 32 years' service.   *Authors' Collection*

Plate 90 (opposite): This class of car, of which there were once 27 represented the latest thoughts on streamlining when they were built for Blackpool by English Electric at Preston during 1934/5. Thirteen were delivered as open-toppers with wooden seats upstairs giving a total capacity of 94. The other 14 had upholstered seats in both saloons and a reduced capacity of 84. Between 1941 and 1942 the open toppers had a lid put on, due to the number of servicemen on leave and civil servants transferred from London who required transport in all weathers. One car, No. 706, *Princess Alice*, has been restored as an open-topper and looks superb, but three others have been dismantled.   *Authors' Collection*

Quite soon after tramway operations started the majority of operators found that there was a strongly expressed dislike of travelling in the open top of a car during inclement weather. Effectively, a 56 seat tramcar became a 26-seater in wet weather, and once a few top-covered cars were available, intending passengers would stand back and wait for a 'dry' car, despite its draughts and lack of heaters. Some tramway managers expressed surprise at this, reasoning that workmen had always walked to work in the rain, failing to perceive that walking at 4 mph is radically different to sitting in a puddle at 12 mph. A few companies, Pontypridd for example, just could not afford to roof all their cars, others like Llandudno were prohibited from doing so as the trams so fitted might blow over. Bristol, for political reasons, never did cover theirs but London was very quick to do so.

Plate 91: Birkenhead Corporation Tramways ceased to operate on 27th July, 1937. Prior to this one reason for their survival was surely their ability to move heavy crowds quickly and in a way that no motorbus ever could. The local football team is Tranmere Rovers and when a home game was playing cars were lined up along Prenton Road West, using a part of the tramway as a car park while service trams turned short at Woodchurch Road. This particular service ran until 29th September, 1934. Apart from being old, noisy and decrepit, the sheer variety of top covers fitted ensured that no two cars were alike by the end of the tramway's life.   *W.J. Haynes*

Plate 92: This Halifax car has a vaguely 'cobbled together' look. The roof is not (as it looks) made of corrugated iron, but when it rained it seems the noise drowned out conversation and the wind buffeting the balconies gave an unpleasant motion. A number of experimental covers were fitted to Halifax cars, varying from canvas and lath to slats which rolled up like a Victorian desk front.

Authors' Collection

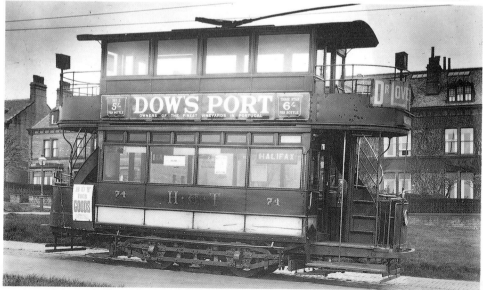

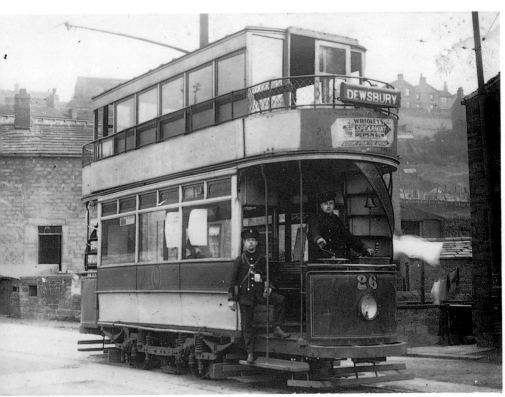

Plate 93: The upper deck cover of this Yorkshire Woollen District car is a prefabricated structure built within the original guard-rails. The trolley mast and pole stuck through a not-very-well-sealed hole in the roof. *Authors' Collection*

Plate 94: All respectable tramcar manufacturers offered 'add-on' tops of varying quality. This is believed to be an offering from Hurst Nelson, but most had to be reasonably light and capable of fitting most designs of cars. In 1925 English Electric of Preston advertised that you should 'Fit English Electric Top Covers to your Tramcars – and protect your passengers during the winter months, the public will appreciate it and your receipts per car will be increased. We can guarantee early delivery and solicit your enquiries.' *Authors' Collection*

Plate 95 (below): An interesting and rare photograph of a 'transitional period' electric car interior. One of 25 cars ordered by Leeds Corporation in 1896 from a local firm, Batley & Greenwood, they were in fact constructed by George F. Milnes & Company of Birkenhead, whose manufacturer's plate is just visible above the left-hand side of the sliding door aperture. Stairs were reminiscent of those used on steam cars and the roof, immensely strong but impossible to wash down, is based on that of a horse-tram. The cushions and curtains which as can be imagined harboured dirt and insect life were quickly scrapped, but the electric lights, however delicate, were a great improvement on paraffin. The vehicle carried 22 passengers downstairs, 29 upstairs. *Authors' Collection*

Plate 96 (right): The progression towards modernity is obvious as the ceilings at least are now smooth and the expanse of glass has made the interior far lighter. This is the interior of a South Metropolitan Electric Tramways car of class 'J' built by Brush in 1906, and refitted with transverse seats in 1928/9, although all were broken up by 1935.
London Transport

Plate 97 (left): Upstairs seating and fittings also underwent a metamorphosis, but the operators always had to bear in mind that this area was frequented basically by working class males and that most smoked. It used to be interesting on certain workings to watch a blueish fog work down the stairs within ten minutes of entering service; the effect of this nicotine on seating materials and panelling alike can be guessed. From 1926 onward the London County Council carried out relatively inexpensive refurbishment of its older cars leading to this improved – 'Pullman' – upper deck seen here on car No. 1817, of class 'E/1', the first of the 1172 cars to be so fitted.
Authors' Collection

Plate 98 (opposite) and 99: Aberdeen 'the Granite City' once had Scottish-designed and Scottish-built tramcars that were the envy of many another city. They also had some interestingly antiquated open balcony cars which were quite marvellous to ride upon on a summer's day, heading for the beach, even if the ladies tished as they fidgeted with their windblown hair and skirts. But the 20 newest cars were built by R.Y. Pickering of Wishaw to an English Electric design in 1949. Steelwork had the seasoned oak framing and green was the predominant colour of the interior. Even the hide covering the G.D. Peters' seats was dyed green and so proud of these were Messrs Peters that they ran advertisements showing their seating in use. Heaters were fitted throughout both decks and the lighting, as can be seen from the photograph, was much improved over that normally fitted. Thirty-eight feet long and 7ft 2in. wide they initially carried 76 seated passengers, although this was reduced later to 74, the transverse seats on the lower deck being replaced by longitudinals to assist passenger flow (and the conductors!). The system closed on 3rd May, 1958 and these fine modern cars were summarily scrapped. Their epitaph can be that they made contemporary buses look shoddy and dreary. *Authors' Collection*

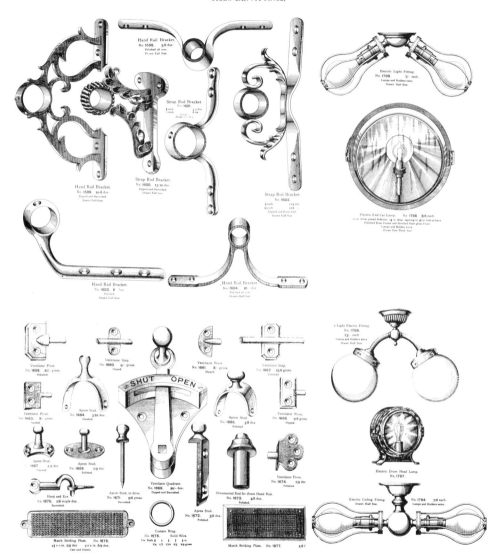

Plate 100: Throughout the history of tramways there have been a number of manufacturers who have specialised in the supply of castings, handrails, light fittings and all the other oddments that make up the tramcar. One of the longest surviving is Gabriel & Company, who started by making brass bedsteads and were entreprenurial enough in the 1870s to see a rising market. In the 1890s they produced a catalogue detailing all the best components that were available, a copy of which has survived, although Gabriel's lost most of their written material when their factory in A.B. Row, Birmingham, was bombed. They still function today, although supplying stainless and DIPTAC (coated) type material for coach and bus use.   A. Gabriel

Tram shelters with varying degrees of usefulness could be found on almost any tram system, although it is worth noting that 'queueing', as we know it, did not enter the vocabulary in its present meaning until World War I. Similarly when electric trams began service they were expected to stop anywhere at any time to suit passengers' whims, as had their horse-drawn predecessors.

Plate 101: Although imperfect this photograph is a rarity for here we have the Crystal Palace in its glory probably just after World War I. The size of the shelter, which also served as an office is indicative of the numbers of passengers expected. Cars Nos. 36–51 of South Metropolitan Tramways were built in 1906, the Spencer hoops were added in 1916, and after some rebuilding, car No. 40 survived until February 1936.   *Authors' Collection*

Plate 102: A far cry from the SMET shelter, Blackpool railcoach No. 621 is arriving at the new 'replica' shelter in Fleetwood. The 'Tramstop' sign is the new Euro model replacing the original Blackpool pattern shown in illustration 104. Car No. 621 (ex-284) was built by Brush at Loughborough in 1937 and, as delivered, had sliding sunshine roofs, sliding doors and full drop windows. Heavily re-furbished over her almost incredible fifty-plus years she remains in service.   *Authors' Collection*

Having abandoned the original idea that tramcars could, and should, stop anywhere to pick up or set down passengers, it behoved the operator to ensure that the would-be passengers knew exactly where they could catch the tram. This sounds pretty obvious, but for many years it was presumed that local passengers knew where to catch the tram and where it went; Birmingham for example had a penchant for signs that read 'To City' and 'From City'. Fine if you lived there, but for a stranger who did not know where he was in relation to, say, Cotteridge, this information was useless.

Plate 103: Liverpool, near the Pier Head (14th August, 1955). *Authors' Collection*

Plate 104: Blackpool's 1930s sign just tells you it is a 'fare stage' – these signs on being replaced were sold for £15 each and avidly snapped up. *Authors' Collection*

Plate 106: By coincidence this stop was at Well Hall Road, rather less than a mile from Shooters Hill Road, but photographed in the Autumn of 1937.

W.J. Haynes

Plate 105: This stop was seen near Shooters Hill Road (Woolwich Common) on 29th June, 1952. Car No. 185 on service 72 is ex-Leyton Corporation class 'E/3'.

Authors' Collection

Plate 107: The most important person in the commercial affairs of a tramway is the conductor, or guard. This official is the one who asks you to 'Pass along the car please', permits eight to go upstairs and five to stand downstairs, who uses an arm to keep excess passengers off the car and who blithely tells you 'There's another one just behind'. This official then rings the bell and goes hunting for fares; they collect money, give the right change and a ticket simultaneously, keep up a cheerful banter, and still get back to the platform in time for the next stop. Well, they did. And still do, on the Isle of Man Tramways, at Blackpool, Seaton and most tramway museums.

Whether it is because the staff are mostly volunteers or whether they are well trained, or just because they have nice personalities is not clear, but like this girl at Crich, the tramcrew of museums seem to replicate the old-fashioned way of doing things. The National Tramway Museum at Crich owes its roots to a collection of cars bought by members of the Light Railway Transport League and their determination to keep these machines as living memories. The Tramway Museum Society was formed in 1955, Crich was discovered in 1959 and, since 1964, when power became a possibility, development has been steady. Now, Crich can rival many of the big tramway concerns' workshops in their activities and output. The girl is on Blackpool 'Standard' 40 which was built in 1926, and arrived at Crich in 1963. The uniform appears authentic and fitting for the service.   *D. Voice*

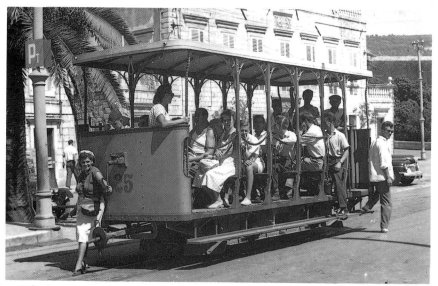

Four girls, four trams, four countries

Plate 108: Dubrovnik Tramways, Yugoslavia. The trailer car is standing at the Old City Gate tram terminus. The power car has been detached from the right-hand end of the trailer and is running round prior to re-coupling at the left-hand end. The cheerful conductress (complete with cash bag) is already holding the electric cable connection in her hand ready to reconnect the trailer to its power car: 23rd August, 1952.
J.C. Gillham

Plate 109: Clare the Clippie answers a query from one of Blackpool's passengers. Like very many of the ticket staff she only sought employment in the summer season, working a double shift and saving as much as she could for the winter time which was to be spent away from Britain. No uniform was provided but she, like most of her kind, was as happy as a lark.
Authors' Collection

Plate 110: Mrs N. Miller was photographed by her husband talking to the crew of this Cadiz car at Balneario Terminus on route 4, then the last remaining tram route. Eight cars were operating the line which ran along the side of a very wide Boulevard nearest to the sea. Motor cars were permitted to play 'Dodgems' in the middle while on the inland side superior modernish trolleybuses plied for passengers. Very continental.   *N.S. Miller*

Plate 111: In June 1960 some members of the Light Railway Transport League visited the Hagener Strassenbahnen in the Ruhr Valley, Germany. The car is No. 52, the location Breckerfeld Terminus and the girl, Fraulein Hedda Neymann, the daughter of the tramway's General Manager, who was acting as the official interpreter. A not dissimilar car can be found at the Midland Bus and Transport Museum, Wythall, near Birmingham, where it is intended to operate a continental-pattern tramway.   *J.C. Gillham*

The Light Rail Transit League (now Association) is the premier tramway enthusiasts' body (whether professional or amateur) and is now best known for its encouragement of, and propaganda work for, modern 'light rail' electric road vehicles. But before the inception of these in Britain there was a long time when the LRTL seemed to be a lonely voice crying in a sea of tramway closures. However, its members kept faith and tried, even in wartime, to continue to withstand what must have seemed a worse enemy than bombs to the tramcar!

Plate 112: Southampton car No. 21 was one of the vehicles expected to pass through the original City Bargate and her roof was purposely designed to allow for the profile of the bar. This pattern of tramcar, nicknamed 'Domes', were officially TCBs (Top Cover Bargate type). No. 21 is seen here in service on 4th April, 1942, the system closing on the last day of December 1949. One destination 'Floating Bridge' was unlike any other on Britain's tramways, but this chain ferry which connected the two banks of the Itchen itself ceased operation after 144 years' existence in 1977. *Authors' Collection*

Plate 113: By contrast No. 843, seen here with a crowd of LRTL visitors in 1952, represented the last and, some say, the definitive Birmingham tramcar. Ordered in May 1929 from the Brush Company, she was completed by a year later with a super lightweight body and bogies, so light in fact that as supplied the gangways flexed when walked on. This problem had to be laid against a weight saving of 4½ tonnes on a standard car. By comparison with another experimental car, No. 842, built by Shorts, No. 843 was unsuccessful, but could have given pointers to a future fleet. She was scrapped in poor condition, July 1952. *Authors' Collection*

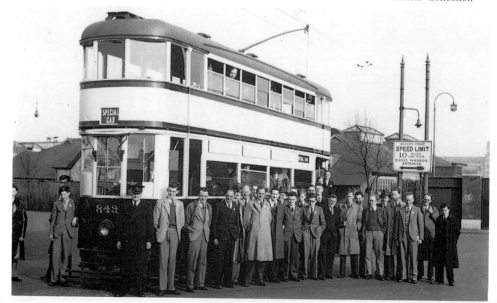

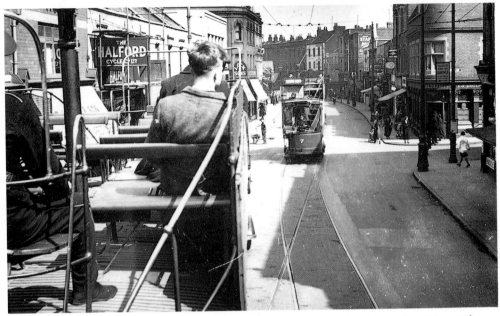

Plate 114: Car No. 7 of the Bristol Tramways & Carriage Company approaches car No. 125 on 17th April, 1939. It is quite incredible to realise just how antique these cars were in comparison with even a London 'E/1', let alone a 1930 streamliner. H.B. Priestley was the photographer in this car.

Plate 115: From a photograph taken by Roger Kidner on 8th April, 1932. The car is standing in The Square, Bournemouth and we are looking south. As befits a seaside town no decency boards inhibit the fresh breeze around one's legs and the ornamental scrolls and finials on the poles remain, but the last car ran exactly four years later on 8th April, 1936. The only consolations are that Bournemouth later had magnificent trolley-buses and their transport museum is well worth visiting.

Decorated cars represented the creativity of the tramways' employees. Although from time to time an excuse for dollying-up cars could be found in major events like a coronation, quite often the basic underlying theme would be put forward by the crews and workshop employees. Thus in Bristol every year a different illuminated tableau was built in aid of the Lord Mayor's Fund for poor children's Christmas dinners, while in Middlesborough the Hospital Appeal Fund was catered for.

Plate 116: Photographs of tramcars being used for wedding parties are surprisingly uncommon, for this was not such an unusual conveyance and in early days was considered quite an up-market thing to do. A prominent shopkeeper or publican would regard the use of a tramcar to show off the bride and her entourage to be proof he had 'arrived'. Nothing much is known about this wedding but the car is a standard Brush built car of The Worcester Electric Traction Company, seen *c.*1910. Assuming nothing untoward happened to the bridegroom in World War I, the bridal couple would have noted the passing of Worcester Tramways in 1928.

Authors' Collection

Plate 117: Pontypridd Tramways were financially never much of an investment, but, at the time of the Coronation of King George V in 1911, there was a resurgence of loyalty to the Crown expressed by means of this illuminated and decorated car. Unfortunately, as a result of some terrible mix-up, most tram crews failed to report for duty on the actual day so that few members of the public were to see the car in all its glory!   *Pontypridd Public Library*

Plate 118: Not all illuminated cars were to celebrate the good things of life. During World War I recruitment of men from all walks of life was pushed ahead at great speed as the early casualties began to mount. Huddersfield used a tram stating 'Your Country Needs You', while Dumbarton's car stressed the importance of joining your 'home' battalion, the 9th Argyll & Sutherland Highlanders.

Halifax sent out car No. 94 (seen here in January 1915) which, as can be seen, appealed both emotively, 'Now or too late', and with an apparent threat, 'Men defend your homes', at a time when there was no likelihood of the Germans wanting to pillage Halifax. Of course, you *should* join the local regiment and be with your mates – the 'Old Pals Battalions'. You entered the Army as a civilian and emerged as a fighting machine, thanks to an illuminated tramcar.   *Authors' Collection*

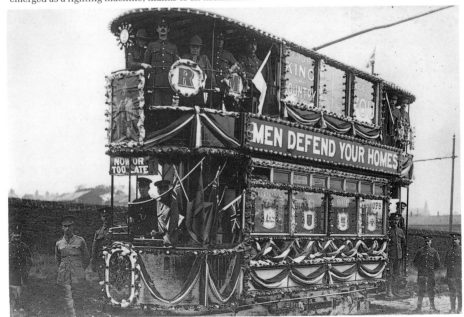

Plate 119: A true cause for celebration! The time and setting: the first holiday in Spring, 24th April, 1905, Glasgow. The Magistrates ordered that all public houses in Glasgow were not to open. Shown here is part of the convoy, believed to have been comprised of 20 or more trams, crossing St James' Bridge at Paisley Cross, the cars conveying 'bona fide' passengers to the watering holes of Paisley. Such was the demand that the last car did not leave Paisley Cross for the City until after midnight.

Paisley Museum

Plate 120: Another cause for celebration led to an illuminated car running in Huddersfield during 1912 and 1913. 'Hurrah for the claret and gold' was the slogan and the cause was victories by the Huddersfield Rugby Football League Club in winning the Rugby League Championship and Rugby League Challenge Cup.

Authors' Collection

Plates 121 and 122: After World War II was over, and the lights could be turned on again, there was indeed a cause for celebration. For various reasons, a lack of material as much as finance, promenade decorations were not restored for a long time. A preview of the Roker and Seaburn illuminations by the members of Sunderland's Town Council on 2nd September, 1949 was supposed to be kept a secret, but by the time the civic leaders arrived several thousand people were gathered to view the 'Scenic Lights', including those on Sunderland car No. 61 shown here both at night and on shed. Built in 1902, she had been rebuilt in 1934 with this rather odd short top cover and more powerful motors. During the illuminations period No. 61 stood at the Seaburn terminus, but the sight of Sunderland's superbly maintained cars normally lit up at night *en route* to Seaburn is also not easily forgotten.

Authors' Collection

Plate 123: Not the last tram, but symbolic of each last tram. Dour Yorkshire scenery, gas lamps, houses and Sykes' Café built from blackened millstone gritstone typify a classical 'tramscape'. The location, West Vale, Huddersfield, looking down Saddleworth Road, is substantially unchanged today, although the café is now a baker's shop and the centre window on the second floor has been blocked up.

The driver, a 'real' tramwayman, shows he is facing a bleak future: either 'the sack' or be required to learn to drive a rubber tyred vehicle. No. 88 for all her enclosed vestibule retained open balconies and had various vicious draughts to deter upstairs passengers. Built in 1913, she was as near a 'Standard' car as Huddersfield had and retained the wooden seats of the period until scrapped in December 1939, when route 7 (West Vale–Almondbury, an unusually long cross-town route) closed. Shortly after 10.30 pm on Saturday, 29th June, 1940, the last Huddersfield tram ran 'on shed'. *W.A. Camwell*

Plate 124: One of the first illustrations in this book shows the opening of Pontypridd tramways and it is fitting that we end with 'The Last Car'. The system was plagued with operational difficulties almost from the start with mining subsidence, an underground fire, flooding, a tornado and excessive snowstorms adding to the normal problems of a relatively ill-financed tramway. Then the Council's bickering prevented through running with the Rhondda Tramways Company between Pontypridd and Maerdy for 11 years. But the final blows were external, the loss of patronage and hence income as a result of both the coal strike of 1921 and the General Strike of 1926, and the ability of the rival Great Western Railway to undercut tram fares, forcing the latter below an economic level. The 30th August, 1931 saw the end and 'The Last Car' whose trolley pole, perhaps symbolically, is held up by a re-wiring bamboo cane. The last manager, Mr A. Armstrong, is the sad-looking gentleman standing by the car. *Pontypridd Public Library*

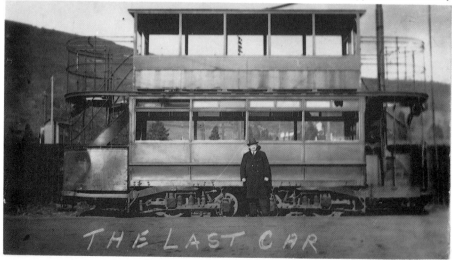

THE LAST CAR